Pieces Of Yesterday

Shayma Zayan

Copyright ©2024 *Shayma Zayan*
All rights reserved.

Contents

Dedication i
Acknowledgments ii
About The Author iii
Chapter 1: Early Shadows 1
The Normalization Of Violence 3
Living Behind A Mask 4
Hiding & Pretending 5
Shadows On Love 6
Final Thoughts 7
Chapter 2: The Fall From Grace 8
Living With Constant Pressure 8
A Never-Ending Cycle Of Fights & Escapes 10
The Extra-Marital Affair 12
Starting Over In Beirut 13
Escaping To Libya 16
Chapter 3: Survival In Libya 18
Arrival In Libya 18
A Loan & A Betrayal 19
Surviving On Pennies 21
Breaking The Cycle Of Struggle 23
Owning Opportunities At Home 23
The Turning Point 24
Chapter 4: A New Life 26
A New Beginning 26
The Strain Of Old Wounds 28

The Weight Of Perfection 31
Fears & Insecurities 32
The Breaking Point 33
Finding A Way Forward 36

Chapter 5: Finding Strength In New Beginnings 37
Healing the Emptiness 38
Losing & Rediscovering Myself 40
Breaking Free from the Past 41
Overcoming Insecurities 45

Chapter 6: Cultural Crossings 48
Experiencing Diverse Cultures 48
The Exhaustion Of Constant Change 49
Health & Safety Concerns in Lagos 50
The Struggles Of Fitting In 51
Dealing with Lies & Infidelity 52
Finding an Ideal Environment 53
The Humbling Impact of Poverty in Lagos 54

Chapter 7: Rebuilding After The Storm 57
The Complicated Grief of Losing an Abusive Parent 58
Healing from Within 61
Pushing Myself to Do My Best 63
Why I Wrote This Book 64
What It Means to Be Vulnerable 66
Letting Go of What You Can't Change 67
Learning to Simplify Life 69

Dedication

To Maya, my beautiful daughter,

You are my inspiration, my joy, and my greatest gift.

This book is for you, a reminder that you can achieve anything you set your mind to.

May your path be filled with love, adventure, and boundless dreams.

Always remember, I believe in you.

Acknowledgments

I could not have written this book without the support of Sophie and the incredible team at Gulf Publishing. Your guidance and dedication made this journey possible.

A special note of gratitude to my dear friend "Casper" – your encouragement and belief in me have been invaluable. This book truly would not exist without you.

I also want to take a moment to honour my younger self – the version of me who fought tirelessly to be heard. This book is more than just a collection of words; it's a reflection of my commitment to face my inner challenges and strive for change, not only for myself but for all those with "broken wings" out there.

About The Author

With humor and a positive outlook on life, I found the strength to face my challenges and fears head-on. From the glitter of wealth to the hardships of near-poverty and back again, I navigated my journey by embracing life's trials instead of avoiding them. This is a story of striving to better myself, not only for my own growth but for the sake of my daughter.

The paths I've taken – both planned and unexpected – have taught me that life isn't about perfection, but about self-discovery and the courage to keep moving forward through fear and adversity. The future remains unwritten, filled with possibilities and new adventures. As I continue this journey, I do so with a clearer understanding of who I am and who I aspire to be. The best is yet to come.

Chapter 1:
Early Shadows

"Out of suffering have emerged the strongest souls; the most massive characters are seared with scars." — Khalil Gibran.

Most people, when asked about their childhood, would share joyous memories that bring smiles to their faces. My story, on the other hand, is quite the opposite – it's tainted with my father's violent and abusive nature.

But this story isn't about that. It's about how I overcame the trauma that marred my early years. It's for those who have been through the same ordeal as me so they know they are not alone in their struggles. I can understand them.

However, before I tell you about how I survived that traumatic life, it's important you get to know me. The childhood me. Writing this book hasn't been easy as it brought back memories I had strived to bury. Memories that I never wanted to relive. It takes a lifetime of work and effort to close the door of your past. Yet, I realized it's important to tell my story for those fighting the same demons. Your struggles may not be visible—mine weren't—but reading about my battles will show you that you're seen and heard. You're not alone.

***

London was a beautiful city where we lived a fancy life right in front of Harrods. To an outsider, it would look like we had everything anyone could want. But behind those pretty places, my childhood was full of fear.

I remember when I was very young, about seven years old. I used to hide behind the sofa because I was scared. My father would get angry and hurt my mother, and I was afraid he would hurt me, too.

When we first came to London, I was in first grade, and my sister was in kindergarten. We used to take the bus to school. But then, my father made it so we couldn't take the bus anymore. My mother or a driver had to take us. One day, my father, who often seemed drunk and scary, got on the bus wearing dark glasses. He yelled at everyone and pulled my sister and me off the bus. We were so scared. He put us in his new Mercedes, and my mother was quiet beside him with my little brother on her lap. It was unusual for him to pick us up; he usually made the driver or my mother do it.

Once we reached home, my mother took my brother and sister by the hand and walked into the apartment. Confused and scared, I didn't know what to do besides following them inside. My father had something else in mind for me, though.

He clutched me by my collar and pinned me to the main door. I was visibly shocked and terrified. And then came the allegations. He accused me of flirting with a boy from my class, even though I didn't understand what he was talking about. He said horrible things about me and called me names.

Being just a seven-year-old, I couldn't figure out why he was so mad. He said a boy's father had complained about me, and that's why he was angry. I was really confused and scared. He punished me by putting me in a basket in the bathroom. Later, my mom told me to ask my dad for forgiveness. Even though I didn't think I did anything bad, I did it because I didn't want more problems.

My father then gave me a long lecture about being a good girl and following his rules. He told me to do my homework and go to bed, but it was hard to focus on anything because of the fear and confusion. He started treating me like I was a bad girl just because I was pretty. He seemed to think that if I looked nice, I must be interested in boys, which made him even angrier.

This was just a small illustration of how we lived at home, always in fear. We always tried to avoid upsetting him. If we make a mistake, we might get hurt. I remember once when I was a teenager, I didn't eat my food, and he rubbed rice all over my face as punishment. We had to be very careful, like mice, moving quietly to avoid his anger.

Happy moments were rare. My parents enjoyed their social life—parties and outings—but for us, those things meant nothing. We had to pretend to be happy when we were outside. At school, we learned to act like everything was fine. But inside, we were always scared and worried.

My sister didn't get hurt as much, but my brother went through the same tough times as I did. We would hide in our rooms when our parents fought, trying to stay safe. We were always listening for footsteps, hoping they wouldn't come near us. Getting beaten up every now and then taught us to walk on eggshells whenever we were at home.

Although we lived luxurious lives in big cities, our lives were full of fear. It's not easy for me to explain how it felt, but what I had to do was pretend to be strong and happy, even though I was really sad.

The Normalization Of Violence

My father made it clear that this was normal, and he told us that if we didn't focus on our studies and didn't get an education, we would end up like our mother —helpless and mistreated. He used her as an example of what we should avoid, showing us what a bad life looked like.

Every day, we saw the violence. He would hit my mother right in front of us, and he was always cheating on her. He even bragged about his cheating, waking us up in the middle of the night to tell us about it as if it was something normal to talk about.

My mother tried to protect us in her way. When she knew my father would come home drunk, she would come to sleep beside me in my bed. This was her way of avoiding him and stopping him from making her cook a late-night meal or worse. But even this didn't always work. Sometimes, he would come and take her away, and we knew she would be in trouble.

Sundays were the worst. My father had a lot of money before, and he would use it to travel. But when he started losing his money, making Sundays even more difficult for us. He would drink a lot, sleep, and then get into fights with my mother. Sometimes, he would throw her out of the house. We would watch as she stood outside, waiting for him to let her back in. We even had to beg him to let her come back inside. If he didn't give her the key, we had to plead with him to open the door for her.

All of this was made to seem normal. The violence, the fear, the shame—it was all presented as just a regular part of life. But now, I see that it was never right or normal. It was a terrible, hurtful way of living that no one should have to accept.

Living Behind A Mask

My mother dealt with my father's behavior by just going along with it. Even though he treated her badly, he gave her and us a very fancy life. We had all kinds of expensive things—cars, jewelry, designer clothes. I had a Cartier watch when I was six and my own BMW when I turned seventeen. My mother drove a Rolls Royce with her name on it and had silverware and clothes from top designers.

She had everything money could buy. I asked her why she didn't just leave him. She had enough money to live on her own and could have gone anywhere she wanted. I suggested moving to a different place, even a war zone like Beirut if it meant escaping her miserable life. But she never left.

Even when my father lost his money and started selling her jewelry and ours, she stayed. It was like she was either too afraid to leave or couldn't let go of him, no matter how badly he treated her. When she finally left, it was because she had no other choice but to rely on us.

She tried to pretend everything was fine, even in front of her family. I remember one time when my uncle came to visit us from Beirut. My father got angry and threw her down the stairs. She had to go to the hospital, and when she came back, she was covered in bandages. My uncle saw her and knew what had happened, but he didn't say anything. He acted like it was normal.

My mother also used us to deal with my father. Instead of dealing with things herself, she made us ask him questions and solve problems. By refusing to engage, she gave us the hard parts to handle. This was her way of coping—by hiding behind us as we attempted to deal with the disorder.

Hiding & Pretending

My siblings and I had different ways of staying safe during the scary times at home. Sometimes, when things get really bad, we would go to our rooms and shut the door. For us, our rooms were the safest spots where we usually hid and tried to ignore all the noise and chaos happening outside. Sometimes, things got really worse, and we would hide under our blankets and pretend we were something else.

I was really good at pretending. I would play music and dance around, pretending to be someone else. Even though I was scared, this act made me feel a little better. I always tried to look happy and hopeful, even when I didn't feel that way inside.

One time, something happened that I still remember very clearly. I wanted to take ballet lessons. I was very young, maybe seven or eight, and all I wanted to do was dance. But my father thought that I wanted to take ballet just to meet boys. Even though I tried to explain that I really wanted to dance, he said no. My mother felt sorry for me, so she secretly let me take one class. When my father found out and saw me in my ballet uniform, he got very mad. He yelled at my mother and hit her, saying she was letting me show off too much.

I also remember a time when my mother's friends from Libya came to stay with us. They were very close to her—a woman and her daughter. One evening, my mother told my father she was tired, and he reacted by hitting her and then urinating all over the bathroom walls. He told her to clean it up, saying she had no reason to be tired since she had everything she could want.

My mom had to clean the bathroom late at night while our guests were there. This is not the end of his violence; these are just some of the many ways my father tried to control and hurt us. We learned to hide, pretend, and find ways to cope, trying to make our lives a little better despite all the fear and violence.

Shadows On Love

The way we were brought up has really shaped our perception of families and relationships. My sister, who is currently over fifty years old, has never had any boyfriends, let alone getting married. Even though she has friends, she has never had any love affairs at all. It's like she's too scared to give it a try.

My brother has been having a tough time with his relationships, too. It's not like he has trouble finding someone – that has never been a problem for him as long as he has money. However, he usually goes out with ladies who are very different from him, maybe in terms of school or how much money they have. It looks like he's finding it hard to meet someone who's just right for him.

As for me, relationships have always been challenging. My marriage ended regrettably. My ex-husband was very distant and uncaring. At times, I felt like it was my fault, even though he cheated on me. When I was growing up, I learned to think that men can't be trusted. My father's actions made me think all men lie and cheat.

Because of this, I find it really hard to trust people or to see the good in them. Whenever I start a new relationship, I get worried about getting hurt. I expect my partner to be dishonest or unfaithful because my dad was like that. I feel afraid and keep my guard up a lot, which makes it tough for me to be in a relationship. If I start feeling too close to someone, I might back off because I'm scared of getting hurt.

I'm trying to change how I see things and be more open to the good in relationships. Right now, I'm seeing someone new, but I get scared and back away at times. My past experiences have had a big impact on how I view love and trust. It's going to take time to change, but I'm working on it. The things I've been through still affect how I deal with relationships today.

Final Thoughts

Whenever I try to reminisce about my happy childhood days, it is difficult because all I remember is my father beating me or punishing me, often when I wasn't even at fault. We lived in great cities like London, Paris, and Monte Carlo, and we had nice houses and other things, but I can't remember any happy moments. Rather, what I can remember are those moments filled with fear or sorrow.

Even though we had fancy homes and plenty of money, our family life was full of worry and sadness. No matter how much we had, it couldn't cover up the fear and pain that were a big part of my growing up.

Chapter 2:
The Fall From Grace

"Family quarrels are bitter things. They don't go according to any rules. They're not like aches or wounds; they're more like splits in the skin that won't heal because there's not enough material." - F. Scott Fitzgerald.

Paris is often called "The City of Light" or "La Ville Lumière." But for me, it's where I faced some of the darkest days of my life. The fear and trauma from our previous homes followed us here, never leaving our side, not on weekdays or weekends.

Living With Constant Pressure

When my father was in town, my parents spent nights at parties, social events, or dinners. When they stayed home, they fought. In fact, they often fought after returning from parties, too, so my mother rarely got any sleep. Perhaps just an hour at most.

On a typical school day, we would hear her dragging her feet to wake us up around 6 am. Exhausted from the previous night's events, she was always on edge, making our mornings just as stressful with her screaming.

Dropping us off at school, she insisted on taking her Rolls Royce—something we always protested against because it made us targets for bullying. Despite attending the elite American school of Paris, our peers bullied us because of our money and cars. We couldn't fit in with the other rich kids; we had wealth but were still considered outsiders.

The journey back home from school always filled us with anxiety when my father was at home. He would send a driver to pick us up, and we dreaded what was to come next. We would find him sitting on the sofa, holding a whiskey in one hand and a book in the other. He was an avid reader, always engrossed in a book.

As soon as we stepped inside, we had to stand in front of him in military style while he bombarded us with ridiculous questions. It was a ritual. While he interrogated all of us, most of his questions were directed at me: 'Who did you see?' 'What did you do?' 'Who did you talk to?' 'Whose son or daughter did you talk to?' He always seemed intent on catching us in a lie. And when he did, all hell would break loose.

But the torture didn't end there. He liked to intimidate us by walking closely behind, so close that we could hear his footsteps and feel his breath on our necks. We never knew his intentions—was he going to hit us? Push us? Punish us? We could never predict what was going on in his mind. Sometimes, we passed his test and entered our rooms unscathed. But often, he suspected me of lying, and that's when the punishment would begin.

He would scream and beat me, yelling, "Who did you talk to? Who did you flirt with? What did you do wrong?" He hit me even when I did nothing wrong. After the storm of his anger passed, he would announce my punishment, which was always the same—being confined to my room.

I wasn't allowed to step out of my room, even for dinner or homework. Everything was brought to me, and at 8 pm sharp, he'd shut off the lights—it was bedtime. This routine remained constant even after we graduated high school. No TV or staying up late past the bedtime he set for us. After sending us off to sleep, my parents would either go out or fight. If they didn't, my mother would wake up at 2 am to make him food because he was hungry.

Weekends were equally stressful when my father was home. He was always on our backs, waiting for us to slip up and make a mistake. Despite being on our best behavior all day, he would often find things to squabble about. I remember how he used to force me to eat stuffed chicken even though I hated it. He would spit on it and make me eat it forcefully.

Weekends were peaceful when he wasn't around. It was the only time we were able to go about our days and nights normally, with ease.

A Never-Ending Cycle of Fights & Escapes

Like I said, my childhood wasn't normal. Neither my siblings nor I were allowed to visit our friends or have them over. We had only one best friend, and that was because our parents knew her family well. Her house was the only place we were allowed to go. It was a relief to be away from our parents' constant fights and arguments, even if it was just for a few hours.

Their fights and eventual reconciliations impacted us in many ways, making us constantly wonder what was coming next. While there were numerous instances where they fought as if it was the end of the world, let me tell you about one time that's engraved in my memory.

However, before I get into that, let me paint a picture of our apartment in Paris. It had a U-shaped layout, so the window in the bedroom my sister and I shared looked right out at the kitchen window.

Returning to the story, my mother was on the phone with my father, who was in Monaco, Monte Carlo. They were arguing about his lack of work. Despite having a lot of money, my father never really worked. It was pure luck that he made a multi-million-dollar deal years ago, and since then, he was squandering it away.

On the call, my mother was warning him that our finances were in serious trouble because we were spending without earning. He had even started selling her jewelry and our cars for extra cash. This topic always set him off, and his anger was predictable.

Despite being drunk, he caught a plane to Paris and came home immediately. We saw him get out of the taxi from our window. Dressed in a sharp white suit, he looked impressive, but his face was twisted with rage. We knew right away that things were about to get bad.

By the time my sister and I dashed to our bedroom, he was at the door, ringing the bell furiously, ready to explode. And explode, he did. As soon as my mother opened the door, he began hitting and yelling at her.

My mother also started screaming, and it was like a constant, jarring noise that always got under our skin. It didn't matter if it was day or night; she would scream loudly, even at 2 am, making sure we knew about the fights. It felt like she wanted us to get involved, to witness their arguments and her distress.

We hated being dragged into their fights, but we didn't have a choice. We were young and scared, so we stayed locked away in our rooms until the shouting stopped. When we did try to step in, we just ended up getting yelled at ourselves. It seemed like the only way to protect ourselves was to stay out of the way and hope the noise would end soon.

That day felt like it would never end. Their fighting dragged on for hours and hours. I peeked through the window and saw my mother chasing my father with a huge knife in the kitchen. I couldn't believe it. Was she really going to hurt him?

In no time, my father grabbed a knife, too, and they were both in the kitchen, facing off with knives. My mother somehow managed to lock him inside, then ran to us. She told us we had ten minutes to grab our most important things because we were leaving. We quickly packed up and left, even though we knew it was just a temporary escape.

For the next few days, we stayed at a luxurious hotel called George V, trying to escape the chaos. During this time, their lawyer intervened, and the police were called to address the situation with my father. He made several visits to us, attempting to talk things over with my mother. We were skeptical that she would agree to reconcile, but to our surprise, she did.

She came to pick us up, and for a moment, we thought we were escaping to Beirut. Instead, we ended up going back home. Incredibly, after our return, it was as though the fight had never happened. My parents took off for Monte Carlo together while we were sent to a summer camp in Switzerland. By the time we returned, everything seemed to have returned to normal, as if the previous turmoil had been nothing more than a distant memory.

It's true that our lives were wrapped in luxury, but we never had a steady income. My father never seemed to work; I never saw him put in the effort to support our family. Occasionally, he'd strike a lucky business deal, but it was never enough to sustain us. We spent what we had, and before long, we were back to struggling. His alcoholism only worsened our financial woes.

I can't recall a time when he was sober. From sunrise to sunset, he was never without a cigarette in one hand and a glass of whiskey in the other. His addiction took a heavy toll on him. He developed kidney failure and, by the age of 70, gave in to various health crises brought on by his persistent drinking. His alcoholism wasted his body and mind, irreversibly damaging it and tearing apart our family. We were always left to pick up the pieces, constantly dealing with the fallout of his choices.

The Extra-Marital Affair

My mother endured until she discovered that my father was having an affair with her best friend. She was a widow with two children, who were as close as family to us.

We were always hanging around at each other's places and going out together as one big family. Over time, I began to sense a particular connection, a strange chemistry, between that woman and my father. I tried to ignore it, pushing the thought to the back of my mind.

I began to notice that she was investing more into her appearance. She was growing out her hair, dressing in clothes that highlighted her figure, and wearing more makeup. It was as if she was trying to look better on purpose, and the uncomfortable truth slowly became impossible to ignore. I also noticed that my father and her were spending more time together than she had been with my mother, which raised some alarms. It all added up perfectly.

I brought it up to my mom, but she brushed it off. She insisted it was all in my head and that there was nothing wrong with her taking care of herself. Although she was in denial, I knew in my heart that something was deeply wrong. It didn't make sense why my father would want to spend so much time with her.

Then, one day, we received a parking ticket addressed to that woman's place. That was the final piece of the puzzle. My mother, still in disbelief, erupted into another argument with my father about his drinking, his financial irresponsibility, and his lack of employment. The fight escalated so much that we were forced to leave home once more and seek refuge in a hotel.

This time, my parents made their private battles public, sharing the details with that woman and their mutual friends and acquaintances. My father declared he wanted a divorce, and my mom said that their marriage was truly over. Even the whole high school eventually caught wind of the drama.

Despite the widespread gossip, the people my parents confided in decided to step in as mediators, trying to mend the rift between them. After a few weeks of chaos, we returned home once more. To our dismay, it felt like we were trapped in an endless cycle, where each solution only led us back to the same problems.

That woman took full advantage of the distance between my parents and grew even closer to my father. Within two years, they were deeply involved in an affair. Not long after, my parents fell into another massive fight, repeating the same old issues. This time, my father lost control completely. The entire family was there to witness his outburst. What started as a minor argument with my mother quickly escalated into violence. He even tried to kill her by smashing a lamp onto her head.

My brother was obliged to intervene in order to calm my father. Once he finally relaxed into his afternoon nap, my mother called the police and we were once again told to pack up our belongings. This time, with the help of the police and a lawyer, we managed to leave.

Starting Over In Beirut

We spent a few days in a hotel while arrangements were made for our departure, including retrieving our belongings from the apartment. When we returned home to collect our things, we were accompanied by a police officer. Seeing my father was surreal. He looked heartbroken as if he was struggling to accept that his marriage had come to such a tragic end.

We bid our farewells and decided to start a new chapter in Beirut. However, by then, my father was indebted to many people, including the banks, and they were growing impatient. The banks seized my parents' bank safes, took away my mom's jewelry and even removed our paintings. We were left with nothing. Even my father didn't pay us a dime.

It was a lot to wrap our minds around. On one hand, we had the pressure of packing up and relocating to another country. On the other hand, we were dealing with mounting financial issues. On top of all that, there was this pain that my father had caused us. It was a lot to comprehend. We were trying to cope with change and loss all at once.

The situation was dire; we didn't even have enough money to buy airline tickets to Beirut. Our checks bounced at the counter, so my sister and I sold our cars. Even then, we fell short, so my brother and I had to sell our expensive watches. It was a tough ordeal, but eventually, we managed to make it to Beirut. As for my father, at that point in our lives, we had minimal contact with him.

However, our struggles were far from over. In Beirut, we faced a whole new set of challenges. I had just graduated from college, my sister had a year left to finish her degree, and my brother was about to start his senior year. With no money, how could we afford their tuition fees? We had sacrificed everything to build a better future, but we had no resources to make it happen.

To help ease into this new environment, we decided to treat our time in Beirut as a kind of vacation—at least until we could settle in. We made new friends and spent some time at the beach, and when fall arrived, we felt ready to confront our problems head-on.

My mother pawned some of her belongings in order to enroll my sister and brother into college and school. By then, we became numb to losing our possessions. My sister lived in a bubble of denial, while I adopted a facade of happiness.

Deep down, though, I knew I wanted more. I was determined to turn our lives around. So, I enrolled in a Master's program with and stood by my mom as she reclaimed the travel agency that my father had bought for her, intended for my grandfather, but left in the hands of my uncle. To our dismay, we found the agency deeply in debt. My uncle had taken out loans from banks without informing my mom, leading to severe financial troubles. As a result, we were scraping by on just $200 a month.

Meanwhile, my brother managed to finish high school and made a few friends. On the surface, it seemed like things were going well for him, but we knew the full story. Unlike other kids who could focus on their studies and relax, we had to juggle part-time jobs and sell whatever we had left to make ends meet.

I sold all my jewelry just to cover the rent, but it was never enough. Eventually, my sister found a job at an Internet service provider office, earning $500 a month. This income made things a bit more manageable for us, but the struggle was far from over.

My mother and I worked tirelessly at the travel agency, but our efforts only went towards covering debts rather than generating any real income. Meanwhile, my brother, at just 17, started trying his hand at business by traveling back and forth to Libya. But what could a teenager really know about running a business? He mostly ended up borrowing money from businessmen, failing to repay them or deliver on his promises. Sometimes things would work out, but often they didn't. He would sell whatever he could and send us small amounts whenever possible.

Our lives had become a constant struggle for survival, and no one knew the full extent of it—not even our friends. We put on a brave face, pretending that everything was fine and that we had no financial troubles.

Escaping To Libya

Alas, how long could we keep up the charade? Our fragile attempts at rebuilding our lives came crashing down when my brother was arrested. His business ventures had landed him in serious trouble, and given his age and inexperience, it was almost inevitable. He was just a teenager trying to navigate a complex world of business, dealing with people far older and more experienced than him.

In a new country where he was still considered an outsider and with no one to turn to in Libya, it was only a matter of time before the police uncovered his dishonest dealings. He was taken into custody due to bounced checks, and part of the issue was that he was acting as the front for my mother. My brother handled everything, which further complicated matters. Even my mother ended up facing a trial because she had signed blank checks.

We were left utterly alone, with barely any money and drowning in debt. There was no one we could turn to for help. The people around us, who belonged to the high social class we once knew, were completely unaware of our struggles. We doubted they would accept us if they knew the truth.

After exhausting all possible options, we hit a dead end. There was nothing more we could do but run. If we stayed, my mother risked going to jail, with numerous creditors coming after her for the money she owed.

I grabbed the only two valuable paintings we had left and, with my uncle's help, took them to a dealer. I sold them for some cash, and we packed our luggage to flee to Libya. It was scary to make our way through the airport. We didn't know if my mother would be allowed to leave or if she was travel banned. There was only one way to find out.

Fortunately, we boarded the plane without any issues. As soon as we were on the plane, I broke down. I was trying to keep myself together through the entire ordeal, but I couldn't endure it any longer. I cried my heart out for the first few minutes on the plane, feeling my heart get lighter.

It was hard to believe this was really happening. We were leaving everything behind once more to start fresh. All we hoped for was that this chapter would mark a new beginning, a new life filled with happiness. And it truly was a fresh start.

Chapter 3:
Survival In Libya

"The journey of a thousand miles begins with one step." - Lao Tzu

Home.

It's a simple word, isn't it? But it's only when you wander from one place to another in search of one that you truly realize its worth. Some describe a home as a place where you feel safe and comfortable. Others say it's a place to create memories with your family and build future wealth.

To us, however, home was Libya. Or at least, that's what we thought when we first boarded the plane to Libya from Beirut. As I mentioned in the last chapter, we had burnt our bridges before coming to Libya. We had no money, no home, and no support. All we knew was that this would be a new beginning, a fresh start.

For some reason, my mother always felt connected to Libya, even though she wasn't Libyan herself. She always liked it there. Perhaps it was because she lived there with my father when they were newly married. It was a time when my mother was deeply in love with my father.

A part of her always romanticized Libya. She believed it was filled with simple people, where she could finally live the uncomplicated life she had long yearned for. She was escaping the chaos of Paris, Monaco, and Beirut, leaving behind her terrible life to start fresh in a country that, to her, seemed simple. That was her only hope—living a life free from stress and turmoil.

Arrival In Libya

The hope of a better life got us through the flight, and when our plane landed, we set foot on Libyan soil, feeling positive about the future. But it was a lot to take in. We were overwhelmed. The airport was crowded with security and people, making us feel suffocated. Where were we supposed to go from here?

My brother picked us up from the airport and checked us into a hotel. It wasn't anything fancy, just a simple and basic building with everything we needed to hit the restart button on our lives. It was the perfect place to start with nothing.

As I said, Libya was a foreign country to us. The people here didn't know us, nor did we know them, so nobody came to rescue us. We had to build our lives independently without anyone's help.

The next month or so went by searching for a place to live. Honestly, none of us anticipated it would be this big a challenge. And why would we? Given my mother's perception of Libya, we thought people here would go out of their way to make us feel at home. If only we had known back then that it was all an illusion.

As reality set in, we realized the people weren't as nice as we had imagined. It was delusional for us to expect someone would hand us the keys to their flat and let us rent it at a low price. Of course, the prices were high. Everyone chased money—a luxury we didn't have at the time.

A Loan & A Betrayal

A few months after we moved to Libya, my uncle, along with his wife and kids, came to visit us all the way from Benghazi. Blinded by belief in blood relations, we thought he was there to help us. Little did we know, he was only there to add to our troubles and stress.

He took out a loan from a man along with my brother and had him sign the paper where the details of this transaction were documented. The paper clearly stated that my uncle would have to pay back the loan in two to three months. My brother, being a naive seventeen-year-old, signed the paper without realizing he was taking full ownership of the deal.

Even though my uncle was around fifty years old, he used a mere teenager to act as the frontman for his transactions. He made sure we didn't catch wind of it, knowing we'd try to save our brother. Imagine the betrayal we felt once we discovered the truth.

We eventually found a small place to live and moved out of the hotel. There, we encountered a new set of challenges. Surrounded by people from a different country and culture, it was incredibly difficult for us to fit in. No matter how hard we tried, we were always cast as outsiders. Being half-Lebanese, we were constantly looked down upon.

It became a nightmare for my sister and me to walk the streets. Our fault? We weren't dressed as conservatively as they wanted us to be. While we wore modest clothes, we could never meet their standards—no matter what we did. Abuse and insults were constantly hurled at us, and in the beginning, it was too much to bear.

Yet, we never lost sight of why we originally came here: to make a life for ourselves. We soon moved into a flat, believing the owner was a nice person. We paid six months' rent in advance and started looking for work. At least now, we had the peace of mind that we wouldn't have to worry about having a roof over our heads for the next six months.

Life never came easy for us, though. We were running out of money and being cheated by people left and right. For instance, let me tell you about the time we lost a thousand dinars to a man who was supposed to fix our kitchen.

Our new apartment's kitchen was a mess, so my mother found a man who could repair it. We gave him the thousand Libyan dinars he asked for, but he never fulfilled his part of the deal. He just took the money.

What could we do? There was no use confronting him or asking for our money back. It's not like we didn't try—we did. But when we confronted him, he started screaming at my mom and even threatened her. So, we were down a thousand dinars with a kitchen that was never fixed. This was just one of the many encounters we had with these not-so-kind people.

Surviving On Pennies

Amidst these challenges, I landed a job at UNHCR—a place where I was never respected and always bullied for my Lebanese origin. The people there never welcomed me with open arms and wasted no opportunity to insult me.

One time, I went to a colleague to borrow his pen. I needed it to sign a paper to get my first paycheck. Needless to say, it was a big milestone for me. Considering the financial situation at home, every dime was precious to us. I was polite and civil to him. But what did I get in return? The man looked up at me and spat, "Do you want a pen or a slap?"

I stood there, stunned. For a moment, I didn't even know how to respond to this insult. I couldn't afford to offend him, though. What if he decided not to release my salary? So, I kept my head down and politely asked for the pen. I was desperate for the money. I needed the cash, even if it was insignificant, just so we could afford to buy food.

I remember we used to go days and even months eating the same food. It was always the same type of small pasta because it was extremely cheap. We ate it for lunch and dinner because that was all we could afford. It doesn't end there, by the way. I have lost count of how many times we had to use toilet paper as tissues because tissues were a luxury out of our budget.

In the meantime, my brother kept borrowing money from people to make our day-to-day struggles a bit easier. How innocent of him to think they would be so kind as to wait until we could afford to return the money. Why would anybody forget about the money they had lent? Naturally, it wasn't long before they came knocking at our door asking for their money back.

It was then that the man from whom my uncle had borrowed money to cover our rent demanded his money back. He tracked down my brother and demanded the money from him. However, my brother didn't have the money. At midnight, with the help of other men, they returned to take my brother away, and he disappeared.

Not knowing what to do, my mother had to get my father involved. Thankfully, my father was able to find my brother and get him released from the man's custody on one condition: he would repay the money my uncle had borrowed.

This triggered a chain of borrowing, paying, and then borrowing more to pay back even more. It felt like we were once again falling back into the cycle we had tried to escape when we came to Libya. The pattern kept repeating itself until my sister finally found a job at a German oil and gas company. That's when things started to look up for us because now she had a stable salary. But we still had a long way to go.

Soon after, I was invited to a wedding where I met and interacted with some people. I got into a conversation with a young and kind lady who worked as an HR representative at Total Oil & Gas Company. She extended an interview offer to me, which I gladly accepted. Fortunately, I was able to land the job, so now my sister and I both had stable jobs and a steady source of income.

With our basic salaries, we tried to stabilize our home life. While the money wasn't a lot, it was enough for us to afford better food and more household supplies. The rent, however, was still a big hurdle for us. Even in Libya, we couldn't make enough to pay our rent on time.

The landlord we thought was nice began growing impatient. After a few not-so-polite reminders, he started threatening us, saying he'd lock us out of the house by putting a chain on the front door. We turned to my brother and father for help, but even they couldn't rescue us from that turmoil.

They believed that fighting their way through every dispute was the solution. But it really wasn't. You can't simply get your way like that. You need to clear your dues; you need to pay. People out there are not kind enough to let you have it all. It's not that simple; it never was.

Truth be told, we suffered so much that our ordeal sometimes felt almost comical. We struggled every single day for months and years. At times, I'd look around and question if this was as good as it was going to get. Was there not a single crack in this window? Would things ever change for the better? Life seemed determined to make sure we never caught a break. It took every ounce of our willpower to keep going and not give up.

I like to think my mother tried her best, but in many ways, she was more like an elder sister to us. We had to take care of her and my dad, rather than the other way around, as conventionally expected.

Breaking The Cycle Of Struggle

I wanted to provide my family with a better life; therefore, I seized every opportunity that came my way. The nature of the job did not matter to me, as long as it was ethical and paid.

That's how we managed to survive. I juggled multiple jobs just to put food on the table until I could stabilize myself at the oil and gas company. My sister did the same. We faced new battles every day, but we never gave up—our circumstances never allowed us to.

While my sister and I worked hard day and night, my brother and father continued the same old patterns of borrowing and repaying. Their life was a constant struggle, and my sister and I vowed we would never live that way. We needed to escape that cycle, so we seized every opportunity, no matter how small. Gradually, we turned our lives around.

Owning Opportunities At Home

It was a long journey that taught me incredibly valuable lessons. Most importantly, I learned that it doesn't matter where you come from or where your roots are—it's all about the strength you possess. You need to stand firm and not let life's ups and downs break you, or people will run over you.

At the same time, I believe it's much easier to rebuild your life in your own country. People often think that moving to a new place—whether it's the US, Europe, or even France—might be the perfect way to start fresh. While it may work for some, it usually comes at a cost: the constant second-guessing because you're in an unfamiliar place surrounded by new people.

You're far more confident when you're in your own country. Even if opportunities there seem scarce, you can truly own them. You don't have to bend over backwards to fit in, secure a residency visa, or find your place among new people and cultures. Committing to grow in your own country gives you the confidence that nothing will stop you. There are no hurdles you can't overcome.

Or at least, that's what I experienced. For the longest time, I was mistreated and disrespected for being half-Lebanese. I did my best to integrate and blend in, but it seemed futile. However, things started to turn around for me when I started showing around my Libyan passport. It wasn't until I started to proudly own my roots and nationality that I found myself more respected and welcomed wherever I went.

I even noticed a shift in how foreigners treated me. Sometimes, it felt like I intimidated them. Why wouldn't I? They were in my country trying to make money, while my sister and I were just as capable and qualified. I had a master's degree and extensive experience from juggling multiple jobs.

The Turning Point

Unlike my brother and father, my sister and I took full advantage of the fresh start life had given us. We worked tirelessly day and night, and eventually, we were able to see light at the end of a very long, dark tunnel.

Although we experienced growth, it was gradual. Over time, we could afford better food and cover expenses we had previously cut back on. Yet, we still struggled to pay rent on time.

One day, the landlord had finally had enough. Despite my mother's desperate pleas for more time, he humiliated her and evicted us in the middle of the night. We were left alone to face this new crisis.

Desperate for help, I called the taxi driver who had been our daily ride to work. He was perhaps the kindest person we had encountered in Libya and seemed like our only hope.

Talking to my brother and father wasn't an option either. They were drowning in debt themselves. I lost count of how many times my brother had been taken away by creditors. He would vanish, and we'd be left worried sick, searching for him. Yet, he never seemed to learn his lesson.

After being evicted from our flat, my father and brother moved us to a small place within a compound for expats. Surprisingly, the rent was relatively low compared to what we had been paying. Plus, being surrounded by other expats made it easier to blend in without feeling like we were starting from scratch.

It soon became clear to my sister and me that we needed to distance ourselves from the rest of the family if we wanted to succeed. We couldn't let them drag us into the same repetitive patterns that had been holding them back.

It was a tough decision, but in hindsight, it was the right one. My sister and I began to thrive in our jobs, earning more money. However, it certainly didn't mean cutting off ties with them. We still hold our mother close to our hearts, and she is our backbone. Eventually, we were able to combine our salaries to afford the rent of a small apartment. It wasn't anything extravagant—just a modest place in a lower-middle-class area on the outskirts of Tripoli. Yet, it felt like a significant achievement for us.

And that was the start of many positive changes in our lives. Our finances improved soon after, and we were able to afford a larger house in the upscale area of Tripoli. It was our home for many years until the 2011 revolution when my family had to flee Tripoli. Eventually, my brother managed to buy my mom two apartments, fulfilling her lifelong dream of owning at least one small apartment. But there's more to the story that you'll learn about soon.

Chapter 4:
A New Life

"Trauma is not what happens to you. Trauma is what happens inside you as a result of what happens to you." – Gabor Maté

There's something about trauma that not many people know or even understand. It has a way of sticking with us, often without us even noticing. It can follow us around quietly and occasionally slip into our thoughts and actions. The worst part is it happens when you least expect it.

We might think we've moved on, we've left the past behind, but do we ever really leave it behind? Sadly, those old wounds have a way of shaping our perspective of the world. And it's the reason why we struggle to trust others sometimes. It can even take the form of anxiousness when things don't go as planned.

Trauma becomes a hidden part of us, influencing our lives in ways we don't always understand. It's only when we start to really look at it, to face it, that we can begin to heal and move forward.

A New Beginning

For the longest time, I believed if I'd attain financial stability, my troubles would disappear. And they did – for a while. I began flourishing in my professional life and eventually became the Head of External & Internal Affairs at Total Oil & Gas Company. And that's when I met my ex-husband.

We had been working on a new name for the company when, one fine day, the HR Head came to me and said, "You need to prepare another invitation for a new arrival from Paris."

The man had just arrived in Libya, and I was supposed to make sure he was accommodated properly. So, I called him and the first thing I blurted out was, 'Are you single?' It sounded horrendous, but in my mind, I only meant to ask if he was to be invited single to the event. Little did I know, this small slip-up was about to turn my life around.

I later met him the same day to settle him into his new apartment. To my delight, he was a wonderful and accomplished man. With blonde hair, green eyes, and the ideal height, I was charmed by him from the very beginning. He was an experienced offshore drilling engineer, which simply added to the list of things I thought were great about him.

Thanks to my little 'blunder', I discovered he was single, and we hit it off as friends straight away. At first, it was fun to spend time together, and before we knew it, we were friends and had a friend circle, which included my sister and me, along with some other expats from our companies. We began spending time at each other's homes for dinners and lunches. That was truly a first, considering how we were never allowed to have friends over as kids.

Initially, it was just us hanging around as friends in a group. We'd go have a picnic at the Roman Ruins like the Leptis Magna and Sabratha. It wasn't long after that he and I started spending time alone together, away from the rest of the group. Soon, we were going on proper dates and acting like a couple. During this time, I had started developing feelings for him.

There was one big challenge, though, that stood in the way of our getting together. He was an atheist, and I'm a strict Muslim. We broke up a few times because we couldn't see how our relationship could work with such different beliefs and cultures. It wasn't about him being French since I grew up in France, and he was very worldly—having lived in places like Algeria, Qatar, and Texas. He wasn't your typical Frenchman who had never left the country. He spoke six languages and was a drilling engineer. He was incredibly educated.

Over the next year, we kept breaking up and getting back together because of these differences. But after our last breakup, I went on vacation to Beirut, and that's when he realized just how much he missed me—and I missed him too. I sought advice from a sheikh, who told me that if he truly converted to Islam and understood it, then we could get married. Without any pressure from me, he decided to take Islamic and cultural studies seriously. He converted, and we eventually got married.

Our marriage was more about deep friendship and love, though later we realized it wasn't the 'in love' kind of love but more of a strong bond of friendship. Still, life was good. We worked and travelled together, and our income tripled, allowing him to open a bank account for me. I could now send more money to my family. Meanwhile, my sister's career was also taking off—she got promoted to a managerial position, and her salary tripled, too. Life started to take a more positive turn for both of us.

And just when I thought I was finally free from the shackles of my traumatic past, it returned to haunt me. Although, now that I think of it, it probably never even left. It was always there with me – the hurt, the betrayal, the pain – silently waiting for the right time to resurface. And it did resurface in my marriage.

The Strain Of Old Wounds

My marriage was nothing like my parents'. It was poles apart, and for many years, my husband and I were actually quite good for each other. The emotional abuse I experienced doesn't even come close to what I went through growing up in my parents' home. But when a person, whether a woman or a man, grows up in an abusive environment, they tend to carry that pain with them into their future relationships. The scars, the cracks, the hurt, the fear, and most of all, the deep lack of confidence stay with them.

For me, this meant that every time my ex-husband was working late or had to travel, my mind immediately jumped to the worst conclusions—he's cheating, something's going on, he's lying to me. There was even a time when he left his wedding band on the bathroom sink before heading out to play squash, which was completely normal for him since wearing it hurt his finger during the game. But instead of seeing it that way, I convinced myself that his intentions were bad, that he was hiding something from me.

I brought a lot of baggage into our relationship, baggage that came from my upbringing and the distrust I had learned from my father. I couldn't trust him at all. This distrust, rooted in my past, clouded my judgment and made me see betrayal where there was none. The wounds of my childhood shaped how I viewed my marriage, and it took me a long time to realize just how much those early experiences had influenced my actions and my perceptions.

I was always searching for cracks in our relationship, convinced that he was hiding something from me. I'd go through his drawers, look at old postcards from past girlfriends, and accuse him of things he wasn't guilty of. In the beginning, he was very patient with me, but over time, that patience turned into coldness and distance.

There was no abuse on his part except for that growing coldness, which in itself became painful. But if I'm honest, I wasn't exactly an ideal partner either. I had my own baggage, and I often let it spill into our relationship. I was aggressive, while he was not. He's a distant, reserved man but never aggressive. My aggression often led to arguments, and though I would apologize at first, eventually, the apologies stopped. Instead, I started looking for things to go wrong, and unfortunately, they did.

As the distance between us grew, he began hiding things from me, lying about small details, and eventually, there were affairs—affairs he always denied, but I knew deep down they were real. It became clear that focusing on these issues would only push our marriage further toward breaking down, so I tried to shift my attention elsewhere.

Then, our daughter was born, bringing with her a whole new set of challenges. He hadn't wanted children at first, preferring to travel and enjoy life without the responsibilities of parenthood. It took me a long time to convince him otherwise, and in some ways, I felt like I had forced it upon him. But when our daughter arrived, she completely changed his world.

Suddenly, this man who had been so distant and reluctant was now deeply connected to our child. She turned his world upside down, and in a way, she brought out a side of him I hadn't seen before. But even then, the underlying issues between us remained, and we had to navigate the complexities of our relationship while adjusting to the new demands of parenthood.

All of his love, his emotions, and his attention were entirely focused on our daughter—completely, overwhelmingly so. I felt sidelined like I no longer existed in his world. This brought new challenges into our marriage, adding to the strain we were already under.

Moving from Libya to various countries as an expatriate with him didn't make things any easier. We lived in France, then Lagos, Nigeria, followed by Qatar, Singapore, and eventually Dubai. Each move added more stress, more baggage, and more complications to our relationship. It was too much—too much of a mix, too many challenges, and I felt like I was drowning under the weight of it all.

Leaving my job was particularly difficult for me. Suddenly, I was stuck at home with a baby, caring for my husband, and though I gave it my all, it didn't feel like enough. I needed more, but I couldn't find it within those four walls.

When we moved to Lagos, the challenges between us grew. I had met my ex-husband as a friend, and I loved him as a friend. I know he loved me too, but maybe we both confused that love—mistaking friendship for something deeper. Marrying him wasn't just about love; it was also a way to change my life. Here was this Frenchman—educated, successful, with a great income and a high position as a drilling engineer. I saw a way out, a chance to create a new life for myself, away from my family home.

So I went for it. But don't misunderstand—I didn't use him or enter the marriage with bad intentions. I genuinely cared for him. But I needed to escape, to change my life, and marrying him felt like the way to do that. It was my opportunity to start fresh and create a life of my own.

My new beginning felt full of promise. Our first year together was a whirlwind—ups and downs, arguments and reconciliations, and so much travel. In those moments, things were good.

The Weight Of Perfection

I had a deep desire to expand our family and become a mother, and I pursued those goals with all my heart. My focus was singular—on my dreams and nothing else. As I mentioned before, it took some convincing, but eventually, he was on board, and soon enough, we were expecting. When our beautiful daughter arrived, those first months in Libya were filled with joy. Surrounded by my mom, family, and friends, I felt at home.

But then, the time came for the three of us to leave and start our new life together. We moved to France for a couple of months and then to Lagos, Nigeria. That's when loneliness began to creep in. I had left everything behind—my job, my family, my friends, my country. I poured all my energy into my husband and our daughter, investing everything I once put into my work and my life into my family.

Without realizing it, I started to become mechanical, trapped in a rigid routine. The baby wakes up at this hour, feeding at that hour, lunch at another, and so on. His work schedule became my schedule—he leaves at this time, returns at that time, and shower at this hour. My days began to feel like a military operation, each moment dictated by the clock, without me even noticing how rigid and repetitive my life had become.

But I felt like the only way to find peace was by seeking perfection. I came from such an imperfect background—my life, my home, my childhood, everything felt flawed. So, I became obsessed with making my own home perfect. This need for control developed into OCD; everything had to be spotless, and everything had to be in order. I expected my husband and our daughter to be perfect, too, and I was relentless in making sure we achieved that. I pushed myself to the brink, working day and night and losing weight in the process, but I was determined to make it happen.

Sure, I had help—a cook in Nigeria, a nanny to assist with our daughter, a driver to handle the logistics. But I took on the weight of it all. My husband began to let go of his responsibilities, trusting me to manage everything, including him. I became his support system, helping him with his work projects, standing by him during rehearsals for presentations, and guiding him as if he were another child to look after.

In the process, I lost the ability to communicate with him as a partner. He was absorbed in his career and our daughter, while I was consumed with maintaining the household and everyone in it. I started to feel more like a mother than a wife, and my frustrations grew. I didn't know how to express myself anymore, so my attempts to communicate turned into arguments—fighting, screaming, because that's all I knew.

He became more distant and cold, withdrawing further with each of my outbursts. I would accuse him of things, and he wouldn't respond. I'd scream louder, but he still wouldn't engage. Instead, he'd retreat into watching TV, focusing on tennis or caring for our daughter. The more we moved from place to place with each expatriation, the worse it got. My need for control, my inability to communicate effectively, everything just spiraled out of control. I realized I needed to find a way to break free from this cycle, but I didn't know how to escape the patterns I'd created.

Fears & Insecurities

During the ups and downs of the oil and gas industry, my husband lost his job a couple of times. When that happened, I stood up for us, using my savings and even selling my jewelry to fill the gaps and cover our expenses. The fear of being without money at the end of the month weighed heavily on me. He had to find work. Fortunately, he was an educated man with a solid career background, so he always managed to land another job. But the fear and insecurity began to take root inside me. I couldn't trust him the way I used to. The thought that he might lose his job again and we could be without income, even for a short time, filled me with anxiety.

Even though he proved time and again that he could find work, my insecurity kept growing. Frustration and stress built up just as our daughter was growing up. I felt like I didn't have a home anymore; we were constantly moving from one country to another, from one house to the next. This constant upheaval began to mess with my mind, feeding the insecurity and fear that were already taking hold. I started to worry about my daughter—was I putting her through the same instability I had experienced? Despite my husband being a good father, I couldn't shake the feeling that our life was unsafe, unstable.

Instead of focusing on finding solutions together, I kept fixating on insecurity and fear. Every time we tried to work things out, I found a reason not to trust the process. I'd think, "No, I don't trust you. I just know something bad is going to happen," and sure enough, things did start to fall apart.

What ultimately led me to leave my husband was a decision that snapped into place one night in Qatar. All those years of fear, stress, and instability had finally built up to a breaking point.

The Breaking Point

What led me to leave my husband? The decision finally snapped into place one night in Qatar. At that time, our daughter Maya was six years old, and we were living in Doha. That year was incredibly tough for us—my husband lost his job for the first time due to an oil crisis at Total, and our house burned down in a fire. It started with the washing machine catching fire, forcing us to evacuate. Shortly after, we had a flood in the same house. It felt like we were cursed with bad luck.

We ended up moving into a furnished residence apartment for the rest of our time in Qatar until he found a new job in Singapore. But by then, I was overwhelmed with insecurity and fear. I felt like I was reliving the traumas of my childhood—wondering if we could pay rent, if we'd have a roof over our heads. I desperately wanted stability, a home to call our own. I kept telling him we needed to invest in a house, but he always responded the same way: "I don't have the money. My monthly income is all we have, and we're barely saving anything, especially with our daughter's school fees."

One day, as I was cleaning out his briefcase while he watched TV, I stumbled upon a bank statement from an account I didn't even know he had. The amount of money in that account shocked me. I confronted him, asking, "Are you hiding money from me? After I gave you all my savings when you lost your job, paid for our daughter's school, and sold my jewelry—are you really hiding money from me?" He couldn't deny it; the evidence was right there in my hand. We had a huge fight, and he left the house.

When he returned the next day, he tried to make amends by suggesting we invest in a home in Dubai. But by that point, something had broken inside me. I realized I couldn't trust him anymore. It felt like I was slipping backward into the same instability and fear I had fought so hard to escape. And in that moment, I knew I had to leave.

I'm going back to my childhood—reliving the fear and uncertainty that I thought I had left behind. My daughter was going to live without a stable home, without knowing if we could pay her tuition. All the traumas of my past began to surface, overwhelming me. I reached a breaking point and told him, "I want a divorce." He pleaded with me, asking for another chance, promising we could invest in a home. But by then, the idea of divorce was fixated in my mind.

We did end up investing in a home in Dubai, and he found a new position in Singapore. We relocated once again, but the notion of divorce lingered between us like a shadow. There was no longer any intimacy, no connection. I knew he was involved in other things on the side, but that wasn't even the issue anymore. My focus had shifted entirely—I needed to find stability for myself and my daughter. We couldn't keep moving from place to place, unsure if we would have a home tomorrow or if he would still have a job. Despite his qualifications as an oil and gas engineer specializing in deep-water projects, I couldn't shake the feeling of insecurity.

Our communication broke down completely. We were just fighting, and I was consumed by frustration and fear. Then, he lost his job again in Singapore. We had to sell our apartment and use the money to pay off taxes and debts. He found another job in Kuala Lumpur, but it meant he was traveling constantly, leaving me alone to manage everything. Essentially, I became a single mom, though he was still technically there.

Ironically, that year in Singapore turned out to be one of the happiest years of my life. It was just my daughter and I focusing on each other and living our lives. I devoted myself to her, helping with her homework and being fully present. I began to realize that this was the life I wanted. I felt a sense of fulfillment, something I hadn't felt in a long time. It was a revelation—being a single mom, even if unofficially, was what made me happy.

When we sold our apartment, we split the proceeds, and I had some savings of my own. That gave me the courage to truly consider starting over, to build a new life for myself and my daughter, free from the instability and fear that had haunted me for so long.

So, one day, I finally told him, "You know what? Let's go through with this. Let's live separately for real." He agreed. He found a job in Dubai, and we moved back there, renting a place. He was working in Oman, coming home every other week. The same pattern repeated, but this time, I was developing my newfound independence, and the distance between us grew.

When he would come home, I could hear his footsteps nearing the front door, and the sound of the key turning in the lock, but the joy of greeting him was gone. Instead of feeling excited, I just wanted to be alone. I knew starting over would be tough—I would need courage, finances would be tight, and I'd have to find work. But I was ready for it.

What I didn't know was that, behind my back, he was hiding money in different bank accounts, pretending he had none while secretly investing and preparing his case for divorce. Then, one day, he left for France and blindsided me by filing for divorce. I was left with nothing. Thankfully, my brother stepped in, hired a lawyer, and covered some of the fees. We went to court for three long years.

During the proceedings, I discovered that even before our marriage, he had investments and bank accounts scattered across the US, Europe, and Dubai—money he never told me about. While I was giving him my savings, he was hiding away his wealth. I was blindsided and shocked. How could the father of my child do this?

Finding A Way Forward

Eventually, we divorced, and I received a bit of money from the settlement. I turned the page quickly, as I always do. My focus shifted entirely to getting my daughter through her International Baccalaureate (IB) program and high school. By French law, he was required to cover her tuition and other expenses, but I still had to manage rent. My brother helped me with that while I started looking for work.

I refused to stay stuck in the same place, spinning in circles of misery. I knew that if I stayed where I was, I would go nowhere. And if I was miserable, my daughter would be too. So, I looked forward, I turned the page, and I focused on my goals. It's one of my survival methods—always moving ahead, always finding a way to turn the page.

And that's really what I advise anyone who feels stuck—don't stay stuck. When you're scared, take the leap. I was scared—scared of divorce, scared of being alone, scared of starting over with just my savings and no monthly income. But I did it because life is short, and I needed to be happy. I needed to stand on my own feet and be independent.

My daughter needed to see me as an example, not someone she wouldn't want to become. All my life, I thought, "I don't want to become like my mother." I never wanted my daughter to feel the same way about me. I wanted her to look at me and say, "I want to be like my mother. My mother is my example, my goal."

I want my daughter to be proud of me, to look at me and see strength, courage, and independence. That's the legacy I want to leave her—to be a mother she can admire and aspire to be like.

Chapter 5:
Finding Strength In New Beginnings

"You may not control all the events that happen to you, but you can decide not to be reduced by them." – Maya Angelou.

It's easy to bring a child to life. Well, it's easier than raising them to be confident, fulfilled adults. What many people don't realize is that children are like mirrors, reflecting the world they see in their parents' eyes.

They pick up more from our actions, gestures, and emotions than from our words. Whether in quiet moments or noisy ones, in the love we give or the hurt we carry, they take in the essence of who we are.

As parents, we shape their inner world, influencing their self-image, beliefs, and dreams. But what if the blueprint we hand down has problems? What if the patterns we've inherited are harmful and trap them in the same struggles we faced?

This is where we have the chance to make a difference. By becoming the person we wish we'd been, we do more than raise children—we help the next generation become strong, free, and whole.

You want your child to look up to you instead of praying they do better than that. It's important to make your children proud of you. However, more important than making our children proud is making that child version of ourselves proud. Imagine looking back and hearing your younger self say, "I'm so proud of who you've become."

That child inside you, the one with dreams and hopes, is who truly matters. When kids grow up without the love and support they need from their parents, they often end up seeking it in the wrong places or from the wrong people.

Healing the Emptiness

I grew up without a strong father figure, and because of that, I found myself drawn to the wrong kinds of relationships and situations, trying to fill that empty space. I didn't get the confidence I needed from my parents; I had to build it on my own.

Even my ex-husband couldn't provide that missing piece—it was beyond his ability to be the role model or support I needed. This isn't just about women; it applies to men, too. Everyone needs that foundational love and support to become their best selves, and without it, we're left searching for something to fill those gaps.

When a child grows up with empty spaces in their heart, they often resort to wrong ways to fill those voids. I can see now that I went through a lot of these wrong places. Reflecting on the woman I was becoming, especially after having my daughter and moving from Lagos to Qatar to Singapore to Dubai, I realized I wasn't proud of her. I got lost along the way. I was so caught up in fulfilling my roles—being a mom managing expatriations—that I forgot who I was.

I threw myself into my duties, making my daughter a goal rather than a joy, and focused on meeting the demands of our ever-changing life. But in all that, I lost myself. I began to dislike who I had become. Looking back over the past 20 years, I see a woman who wasn't true to herself. I wasn't fond of her, and I certainly didn't want to remain that person.

I wish I could have told my younger self to be strong, to pursue what she truly wanted, and to assert herself. Instead, I just went through the motions, meeting the immediate needs of my family and neglecting my own needs.

The trauma and uncertainty only deepened the voids inside me. I wasn't filling those gaps; I was falling behind, not moving forward. My daughter, while she showed me the essence of love and what it means to be a mother, couldn't fill those voids for me.

That's when I realized I needed to find a way to reconnect with myself, to become someone I can truly be proud of—not just for me, but for my daughter and the little girl I once was. Now, I feel like I'm finally getting closer to who I always wanted to be. Looking back, I realize that before, I was just going through the flow, focusing on everyone but myself, losing myself in the process. It was especially hard during our moves to Lagos, Qatar, and Singapore. I was so caught up in managing everything that I didn't truly connect with her.

But things started to change in our last year in Singapore. In a way, it helped us to be alone together – it gave us a chance to grow closer. And by the time we relocated to Dubai, we had a stronger bond. I was no longer just a mother fulfilling her obligations. It was more than that. Deeper. I was her friend, her best friend.

I have always wanted to be entirely opposite of my mother. Not that she wasn't good enough or I didn't love her so. It's just that she had a difficult life, and she was often overwhelmed. Issues with my dad never really left her mind that she could focus elsewhere. As a result, we were often left feeling neglected. Sure, our other needs were well taken care of back when we had everything. But emotionally? That's a completely different story – we were always deprived of our emotional needs. There were countless times when I wished my mother was there for me. Sometimes, I'd crave her presence for something as mundane as taking a bath or brushing my teeth.

I wanted to be a different type of mother. I vowed to be there for my daughter at all times. Nothing was more deserving of my time than her.

Breaks were completely out of the question unless she was with my mom or family. Only then would I go on a vacation or hang out with my friends. Truth be told, it was quite challenging. Yet, I wanted my focus to be on being present for her. And it did work out for the best in the end, as we have the best mother-daughter bond now.

Losing & Rediscovering Myself

Granted, I might have been a bit suffocating at times. But I was merely trying to give her everything I couldn't have as a child. I was present and attentive. I was a mother to her just as much as I was a friend to her. However, in doing so, I lost sight of myself while facing my own struggles.

Back in 2011, during the upheaval of the Arab Spring, when Muammar Gaddafi was overthrown, my family's life was turned upside down. My mom, sister, and brother fled Libya and moved first to Dubai, then Istanbul, and later Tunisia. My brother was building his business empire, finally achieving financial success, while my sister rose to a prominent position in a German oil and gas company, shuttling between Germany and Istanbul.

My mom's dream was to have a secure home, and my brother made that happen by buying two beautiful apartments for her putting them in her and my sister's names. Their lives took a dramatic turn for the better. Meanwhile, I was struggling, but they would invite me to join them, and my daughter enjoyed luxurious trips with them each summer, traveling from Istanbul to Monte Carlo, Cannes, and Bodrum. I wanted her to experience that world, even as I feared the uncertainty of it all—what if my brother lost his wealth or faced challenges?

My mom shared those fears too, but she took them even further. We'd often have to remind her to focus on the present and be grateful. We would urge her to move on from our past hardships—no more dwelling on times when we had nothing or had to make do with less. We wanted her to enjoy the life we had now rather than being haunted by what we once lacked.

Despite my best efforts to move forward, my mother always seemed to pull us back into the shadows of our past. She couldn't help but bring up old traumas that we were all trying to forget. At times, it even felt like she was never truly content with all the good things happening to us.

For instance, if she was in Istanbul, she'd want to go to Tunisia. And when she was in Tunisia, she'd long for Istanbul. It was difficult to keep up with what she wanted. My brother was giving his best, making his business grow and growing financially. Even my sister was stable and successful. My mother had apparently no reason to worry. Yet, for some reason, she was always apprehensive about what the future held for us.

She would stay stuff like everything will eventually fall apart. We didn't get it. Things were going well, weren't they? But this constant sense of impending doom made us question it all as well. It was becoming increasingly difficult to enjoy the life we had built for ourselves.

Breaking Free from the Past

I knew I needed to break free from this mindset. It wasn't good for me; it wasn't good for my daughter. If I wanted her to live a life that was different from mine, I had to keep myself from living in constant fear of disaster.

I wanted to create a life for her where she could appreciate the good things around her. Not one where she'll always be waiting for the next bad thing to happen. And the only way I could make that happen was by escaping the negativity around me.

My religion offered a sense of peace during this challenging time. Honestly, I've always been religious, like my mom. In fact, she's more devout now than she used to be at a relatively younger age. Observing her has truly shaped my understanding of faith, and it's my goal to instill the same principles in my daughter. I really hope for her to find the strength that religion has given me.

In my opinion, Islam is a guiding light. If it wasn't for it, I'd be lost with no strength, morals, or a sense of direction. But whenever I'm feeling down, I turn to prayer and the Quran. The teachings in there are a source of comfort, purpose and guidance. In fact, it even pushes me to become a better purpose so I can attain my ultimate goal of entering paradise.

However, even though I find support in my faith, I've struggled with valuing myself. If anything, I always thought I was the least valued than my siblings. I never received the confidence or recognition I needed from my parents. Even when I deserved it.

For the longest time, I felt inadequate and not good enough. Proving my worth was always an impossible battle. A battle that I could never win. Although my faith helps a lot, there are days when some parts of me struggle with these insecurities.

Growing up, I was constantly told by my father that if I had good looks, men would only want to play around and have fun, never genuinely interested in me. He used to say we were never tall enough, smart enough, or good at anything. Especially me—he made me feel like I was good for nothing. These words took a toll on me, and I never really valued myself. I struggled to believe that anyone could truly love me.

So, when a man or even a young boy showed interest in me later on, I was surprised and flattered. I would think, "Wow, someone actually likes me!" My mind would race with thoughts of, "Does he really care about me?" Even though deep down, I knew that just because someone showed interest didn't mean they genuinely cared, I still felt grateful for the attention. It was like a small validation that I mattered, even though I wasn't sure why I felt that way.

The feeling of not being enough followed me into my marriage as well. My ex-husband never truly showed me the love and respect I needed, but my family and others would often remind me that I should be grateful for him. They'd say he was so much better than me—more educated, with better manners—though I had my own strengths.

I internalized this and let myself believe I wasn't worthy, accepting less than I deserved. I carried on with this mindset, trying to make the best of things while feeling like I was always falling short.

My close friends used to tell me, "Wake up, value yourself, love yourself." At the time, I'd get offended. I felt like I did, but deep down, I didn't truly believe it. They'd insist that once I could look in the mirror and genuinely say, "I'm worthy of love and respect," my life would start to change.

But life, you see, never came easy for me. And my insecurities were too deep-seated that they almost ruined a beautiful relationship for me.

Back in 1999, on the eve of the new millennium, one of my best friends was celebrating her engagement to an Egyptian man. The night was filled with excitement as friends from Cairo had come to Beirut for the occasion. But for me, the night was anything but festive. I was down with the flu, feeling miserable and convinced that I looked awful.

Yet, I couldn't miss my best friend's big night, so there I was, sitting at the table, grumpy and trying to survive the evening without paying much attention to the world around me.

Just then, my best friend approached me with a mischievous smile. She insisted I meet a young man who's Libyan. Naturally, I recoiled – it was an instinct. My prejudice kicked in, and I firmly told her I had no interest in meeting him.

But she persisted, describing him as cute and charming. Despite my protests, she dragged me across the room, and before I could escape, there he was—a man with a flirtatious smile that told me he was used to getting his way.

He came from a prominent Libyan family, was wealthy and well-connected, and lived in Cairo. He had an air of confidence, almost arrogance, that initially put me off. I was determined not to fall for his charm, but despite my best efforts, I found myself intrigued by him.

We spent time together in a group, and little by little, I realized I was falling for him. He, too, seemed genuinely interested in me. He took my number and called me often, and soon enough, I started developing feelings for him despite the defences I had built up.

After a whirlwind few days in Beirut, he returned to Cairo, and we continued to stay in touch. But then, the calls became less frequent, and eventually, they stopped altogether. My insecurities flared up—was it because I was only half-Libyan? Did I not measure up to his expectations? I was hurt, and my pride kept me from reaching out.

Months later, we were back in Cairo for my best friend's wedding. I hadn't contacted him, determined to move on. But as I stood watching my friend dance with her new husband, another friend nudged me and pointed out that he had just arrived.

Before I could gather my thoughts, there he was, standing in front of me, asking what was wrong. I tried to play it off, but he saw right through me. I told him I had to leave early, and without revealing where I was staying, I said goodbye and returned to my hotel.

The next morning, just as I was getting ready to leave for my flight, the hotel room phone rang. To my surprise, it was him. He had stayed up all night, calling every hotel along the Nile until he found me.

He insisted on taking me to the airport, and I reluctantly agreed. Over breakfast, we talked, laughed, and, despite everything, I couldn't help but forgive him. When we said goodbye at the airport, there was a sense of something unfinished between us, a connection that lingered even after I returned to Beirut.

Over time, his habit of disappearing from my life continued, and my insecurities only deepened. What I didn't know was that his family had faced a series of misfortunes—his father's business went bankrupt, and he suffered a stroke.

He had been dealing with immense pressure, trying to rebuild his family's business and stand by his father's side. But without communication, all I felt was the growing distance between us.

Years passed, and our paths would occasionally cross, sometimes unknowingly. We later realized that we had been in the same places at the same time, but fate had kept us apart. He eventually married a Libyan woman, and I returned to Libya, where our lives took different directions. But even then, he was always in the back of my mind, a lingering memory that never quite faded.

Then, in the summer of 2021, out of the blue, I received a friend request from him on Facebook. We reconnected, and it was as if no time had passed. We spoke every night, reminiscing about the past, and he shared with me the challenges he had faced over the years—his marriage was falling apart, and he was still struggling financially. We opened up to each other, and it was clear that the feelings we had once shared were still there, stronger than ever.

When we finally met again in Cairo, it was as if the years melted away. We knew, without a doubt, that we were in love. But I told him I couldn't enter into a relationship until he was free and independent.

He asked me to be his second wife, and although I hesitated, I couldn't deny how much I loved him. I agreed, understanding the responsibilities he had toward his children and his desire not to break up his home.

But as time went on, the weight of his financial burdens and his unresolved marriage issues took a toll on us. We argued and drifted apart again, not speaking for the rest of the year. It wasn't until misfortune struck him that I reached out with a simple message of comfort.

His response was immediate, quoting a Japanese saying: "If you cannot stop thinking about someone, it means they feel the same way." I tried to ignore it, but my conscience wouldn't let me. I finally responded, and when he called, the first thing he said was, "I feel like my soul has returned to me just by hearing your voice."

We spoke about everything, and despite the unresolved issues, I knew I couldn't let him go. We met again, and this time, I agreed to wait for him—to wait until he could stand on his own, until his children were settled, and his life was in order. We became engaged and committed to each other but kept our relationship pure, waiting for the day when we could truly be together.

Overcoming Insecurities

It wasn't until after my ex-husband left that I got a wake-up call. The way it impacted my daughter, who was only 14 then, was alarming for me. She came home one day, tears staining her face, and said, "I lost my father."

I was as shaken as any mother in my place would be. To comfort her, I made up stories about a job offer or other excuses. But she was a smart kid; she knew better. The absence of love and value didn't go unnoticed by her. And truth be told, it was heartbreaking. It shattered me to see my own daughter developing a void I have lived with my entire life.

That's when I knew. I have put aside my issues with self-worth for far too long. It's time I finally confront them and begin my healing journey. It wasn't just something I needed to do for myself; it was for her as well.

My daughter is an incredibly beautiful young lady—smart, intelligent, and a top student who graduated as valedictorian. Now she's studying at one of the best business universities in Europe. With her mix of European and Middle Eastern beauty, she's got this striking look with her brown hair and hazel eyes.

Despite all her achievements, she seems to attract men who don't take her seriously – men who are more interested in playing games. I noticed this pattern starting when she was around 13, turning 14, and it's continued since then.

I always tell her to value herself and wait for the right person, but it feels like she's stuck in a cycle. She started going out more, trying to fit in with girls who didn't have the best reputations. I didn't want to impose too many boundaries because I remember how stifling it was growing up in a strict household. I wanted to be her friend, not just her mother. So, I let her have some freedom—coming home at a certain time, offering advice, and keeping an open heart.

For the past few years, I've been trying to mend the gaps left by her father's departure. I've done my best to pick up the pieces and fill the void he left behind. It's been a heart-wrenching journey, watching her struggle and trying to guide her without judging, hoping she'll find her way to someone who truly values her.

Even though my ex-husband, her father, continued to visit her, offering advice and support and helping her through tough times, I realized that I needed to be the example she looked up to. Seeing her struggle made me confront my own issues. I understood that if I wanted her to value herself, I had to start by valuing myself.

That realization was a turning point for me. I got serious about finding work, took control of my life, and finalized my divorce. I wanted to show her that her mom loved herself and was worthy of a good man. More importantly, I needed her to see that she, too, deserved the best. I wanted her to know that she was even more deserving of love and respect than I was.

In her senior year, something amazing happened. I saw her start to truly value and love herself. She entered a serious, stable relationship with a great young man from a good family, and the change in her was incredible. This wasn't just a big step for her—it was a huge moment for both of us.

Our journey together became a team effort to fill the gaps left by her father's absence. I realized that to show her how to value herself and find a good partner, I needed to do the same for myself. I wanted to break the cycle of emptiness and self-doubt that had been a part of my life. By working on myself first, I aimed to give her the strong foundation she needed to become the confident, amazing young woman I always knew she could be.

We faced our struggles together, and I was determined to ensure she wouldn't have to deal with the same challenges I did. I wanted her to grow up knowing she deserves love and respect and that she can achieve everything she dreams of. Seeing her grow into this strong, self-assured person was everything I hoped for—and it marked a new chapter for both of us.

Chapter 6:
Cultural Crossings

"It is not our differences that divide us. It is our inability to recognize, accept, and celebrate those differences." — Audre Lorde.

Everyone desires and deserves a better life. We often go to great lengths to try to achieve it. We switch jobs, relocate to better neighbourhoods, or even move from country to country—all in an attempt to leave our past traumas behind and build the life we've always dreamed of.

However, what would you do if you woke up one day and discovered that the dream of moving to another country was not all that glamorous? Starting fresh in a new environment comes with its fair share of price. The price of leaving behind everything that's familiar to you.

A new place, new people, new environment; it demands time and patience in order to adapt to a new life.

Initially, it's exciting to explore a new environment, but it surely fades away once you encounter the challenges of adapting. The uncertainty of the unknown quickly takes over the comfort of old routines, familiar faces, and the ease of understanding a known culture. In fact, even the simplest tasks, like finding your favorite food, can become complex when you're in an unknown place.

Experiencing Diverse Cultures

I've lived in many different cultures throughout my life—European, African, and Asian. Each has its own customs and values, but one thing remains constant: none of them accept domestic violence as normal or acceptable. Domestic violence is universally destructive; it shatters a person's self-worth and confidence, making them feel small and powerless. No culture condones this kind of harm.

Yet, despite this universal understanding, the reality is that many people remain silent about their suffering. When I encounter domestic violence or hear about it, I try to intervene and offer support, but often, those who are affected are reluctant to accept help. They close themselves off, retreating into their private struggles. It takes immense courage to speak out about experiencing domestic violence because it attacks the very essence of one's identity.

As an Arab, I hold my own culture close to my heart. It shapes my values and identity. But no matter where we are from, the pain inflicted by domestic violence is a common thread that transcends cultural boundaries.

I had a difficult time in Singapore. It was a very challenging experience, and I felt lonely and isolated. I was alone with my daughter and didn't have any friends to rely on. Singapore seemed less diverse compared to other places like Lagos, Qatar, or Dubai, where people from all over the world live.

Lagos is a cultural melting point. It's a diverse country, filled with people from all around the world that settled in Nigeria due to its high economic opportunities. In that aspect, its cultural diversity is a common feature with Qatar and The United Arab Emirates.

However, Singapore was different. I felt alone with my daughter, and there weren't many opportunities to interact with others. The culture didn't align with my interests, and the most frustrating part was feeling like I was adapting to the new environment all by myself.

The Exhaustion Of Constant Change

When you move to a new place with your partner, you imagine you're a team, and you'll be tackling the challenges together. But for me, it felt like the opposite. My husband was often absent, and I was left to handle everything—caring for my daughter, managing the household, and dealing with all the responsibilities on my own. The weight of it all was exhausting and made the experience of expatriation even more difficult.

Now, living in Dubai at an older age, with my daughter having graduated, I can finally say I'm not exhausted anymore. I've taken control of my life, and it feels like a new chapter.

But reflecting on those twelve to thirteen years of expatriation, I remember how draining it was. Each move, each new culture, felt like a never-ending cycle of starting over. I was always on my own, handling it all.

During those years, my daughter was always the priority. As a mother, my focus was on her well-being. Moving from one country to another, leaving behind friends and familiar places every few years, was tough on her. Every new place was different, often more extreme than the last, and it was my job to make each transition as smooth as possible.

Upon arriving in a new country, my first priority was to ensure my daughter felt settled. Setting up her bedroom and taking care of all her needs came first, as I wanted her to feel at home as soon as possible. I wanted to create a sense of continuity. A bridge to cover the gap between her previous home and the new one.

It would break my heart if she ever woke up and said she didn't want to go to school. I was always preoccupied with her feelings and needs. Is my child happy? Is she safe? Is she okay? I would keep asking myself these questions as she was the most important person in my life. I needed to ensure her room was cozy and her surroundings were secure.

Health & Safety Concerns in Lagos

From all my expatriations, the most difficult one was Lagos, Nigeria. It was the most challenging due to the high risk of safety and health. Lagos was infamous for kidnapping, especially the employees of the oil and gas companies. The kidnappers targeted the women and children along with the employees. This was because the oil and gas companies paid instantly and never challenged the ransoms, in order to ensure the safe return of the children, women and employees.

One incident that stands out is when we were relocating from Paris to Lagos. There was a news report about a British man employed by BP, the British Oil and Gas Company, whose two-year-old daughter was kidnapped. The kidnappers demanded a million pounds for her release, which BP paid. I couldn't shake the image of the happy parent hugging his child after her safe return.

Before arriving in Lagos, we underwent training provided by the oil and gas company on how to handle ourselves when surrounded by motorcyclists, a common strategy used by kidnappers. The training was rigorous and emphasized the importance of being alert.

If ever surrounded by motorcyclists, the best course of action was to comply with the abductors' demands. It was advised not to resist, and the driver or security should surrender whatever the assailant demands to avoid a potential shootout. I remember the story of a lady, the wife of a German businessman, who was shot during a similar encounter. This was the harsh reality of living in Lagos and other cities in Nigeria.

My priority was to protect my daughter. I was always with her from the morning drop-offs to nursery and pre-kindergarten to all her activities. I was always with her, holding her hand.

My daughter's health was a major concern, as she was sick one week out of every two, with fevers reaching 39 degrees. Taking care of her health, safety, my husband, the home, and the staff was mentally exhausting. I prioritized taking care of myself last, and now I wonder if it was worth it.

The Struggles Of Fitting In

When I arrived in Doha, Qatar, in 2011, the environment was noticeably different. It was a male-dominated society, and people were more narrow-minded than they are now. I felt isolated and found it hard to connect with others. Dealing with the challenges of living far from home was demanding, but my main focus was on my daughter and helping her adjust to each new place.

We had relocated from Lagos, Nigeria, where music filled the streets and people danced at 5 o'clock in the morning, to a completely different, solitary place. The house we lived in was old and had issues, such as frequent flooding. Life was challenging, particularly after my ex-husband lost his job.

When we moved to Singapore, the loneliness became even more pronounced. I was solely responsible for ensuring my daughter's happiness and comfort. My attention was on her well-being, her room, and her schooling, yet I increasingly felt alone. His absence made everything even more difficult.

Stress was constantly present, especially when adjusting to different cultures. I strived to set a good example for my child, demonstrating that it's okay to embrace change and be adaptable, but I needed to adjust first. If I wasn't content or adaptable, she wouldn't be either.

The first three years in Singapore were especially tough. While my daughter was doing well at school and making friends, I felt lost. I was struggling to fit in and often felt like I was just fitting out. It was a difficult balancing act, trying to stay positive for her while dealing with my own feelings of isolation.

Dealing with Lies & Infidelity

I first caught my ex-husband cheating with our part-time maid in France. We had a young French woman come in three times a week to help with deep cleaning. One day, I was in my room when the doorbell rang. I saw him answer the door and let her in. I walked into the hallway and saw her kiss him. I was stunned.

I asked him what was going on. He tried to convince me I was imagining things, saying it was just a friendly hello. But a kiss isn't how you say hello to your boss, and she was let go immediately. I didn't bother discussing it with her.

We moved on from that and then came Lagos, Nigeria. It was a tough period for me; I was so stressed I lost weight and fell to 39 kilos. My daughter, who was only two or three years old, was also getting sick. We decided to take a month-long trip back home to Libya to regroup.

When we returned to Lagos, one night after putting my daughter to bed and giving her milk, I had some free time on my hands. The cook was still busy in the kitchen preparing dinner, so I thought I'd take the chance to go through some family photos. I was lost in memories and hadn't realized how much time had passed while I was flipping through the pictures.

Then, I stumbled upon a picture of my ex-husband at a bar. In the photo, he was hugging two blond women, and it was clear from the context that it wasn't an innocent encounter. I felt a wave of frustration as I turned off the old computer screen.

When he walked in, I confronted him, saying, "So, these are your new best friends?" He brushed it off, claiming it was nothing and didn't mean anything. By then, I was beyond fed up. I told him to go take his shower while I cleaned the kitchen and prepared dinner. I wanted to keep things calm, especially since my three-year-old daughter was asleep nearby.

As he sat down for dinner, he said, "I need to tell you something. Please don't be mad or offended." Curious, I asked him what it was. With a straight face, he told me, "I put your head on their bodies."

I was speechless. I did not know what to say. I was truly stunned.

Finding an Ideal Environment

Of course, when you're moving to another country with your children, safety and health are your top priorities. Hence, Singapore seemed like a good choice to me. The country had a safe environment and well-maintained health standards.

Even the school systems there were exceptional. Besides, the organized and clean culture of the Singaporeans aligned with my own values. Now that I look back, it was truly an ideal place to raise a child. Dubai was also a dream to live in due to the same reasons.

On the other hand, my stay in Qatar was challenging from a health standpoint, even though it was safer than Lagos. In 2011, the healthcare system in Qatar was not as developed, and the dusty environment posed additional health challenges. Nevertheless, Qatar still provided a certain level of safety that was better than Lagos.

Lagos, on the other hand, was a struggle in terms of both health and safety. The improvements in these areas from Lagos to Qatar, and then from Qatar to Singapore and Dubai, were significant. The focus on safety and health in these later locations made a world of difference, creating a much more secure and healthy environment for my child and me.

The Humbling Impact of Poverty in Lagos

I've always been a humble person by nature, though I'm also quite extroverted yet reserved. Libya didn't particularly make me more humble, as the people there often exhibited a lot of self-confidence and sometimes even superiority. However, it was the streets of Lagos, Nigeria, that truly humbled me.

In Lagos, I saw things that were deeply moving and eye-opening. There were children who knew no other way of life than to use the streets as their bathroom. It was entirely different to the luxury I experienced.

We lived in a gated community mostly populated by employees of foreign international companies and oil and gas companies. From our balconies and windows, we could see the poverty surrounding our area. As I cleaned the dishes at my kitchen window, my view was of a shack where the man's tub and toilet were located in his backyard. There was a stark contrast between the two classes of society – the rich and the poor. It was so obvious and a part of everyday life. People became immune to the poverty around them, sometimes choosing to look away as if it didn't even affect them anymore. It became a way of life.

Living abroad made me realize how privileged I am, and witnessing such poverty was an eye-opener. It helped me reflect on how the other half lives and made me more grateful for what I have. It also made me more independent and accepting of the fact that my marriage is not flawless, and

I have a daughter to take care of. I wanted her to be strong-spirited, multicultural, and have a good emotional IQ, and this drive empowered me to be strong for her, even though I didn't feel that strong at the time.

By the time we arrived in Singapore, I had come to terms with the lies and deceit in my marriage. My ex-husband's actions made me tougher. I became immune to his lies and infidelities. I learned to see through his pretense.

The turning point of my feelings towards my ex-husband occurred one day in September 2017. We were in our second year in Dubai, and my daughter had begun middle school. I naively began to feel settled and happy, genuinely believing we were on a secure path. One day, I asked my ex-husband for papers that I needed from his company in order to renew my helper's residence visa.

A day turned into a week, and then into a month, and I realized he was strangely buying time. One night, as I was cleaning the dishes, he bluntly informed me that he was made redundant back in the month of June, that our residence visas were cancelled, but he assured me not to worry.

I was too stunned to reply or talk to him at all. In fact, this was the point at which I stopped talking to him at all, losing the small amount of trust I had left in me.

Whereas I thought he was waking up early to go to work, attend meetings, spending time on the offshore rig, and gain an income, he was spending all his days until the evenings in a rented office looking for a new position. Whereas I thought we were living legally and securely, we were not. In fact, I had been living in an illusion.

It reached a point where I knew I couldn't go on like this without losing my sanity—and risking my daughter's emotional stability. That's when I decided to ask for a separation. Was it easy? Oh, not at all. But was it necessary? Absolutely.

He dragged out the financial problems, claiming we'd get divorced in Abu Dhabi, while he secretly built his case and eventually blindsided me by leaving for France to file for divorce. Despite the chaos, these experiences made me stronger.

Living in expatriation, I learned to survive, choose my battles wisely, and adapt to new cultures. My main focus was always on creating a stable environment for my daughter, even when everything around us was falling apart. I had to find excuses to cover up the arguments and fights until there were no more excuses left to give.

All these heartbreaks, illusions, and harsh realities made me strong. I had to stand firm and move forward, not just for myself but for my daughter's sake. It was survival mode, and everything I did was for her well-being.

Chapter 7:
Rebuilding After The Storm

"There is no greater agony than bearing an untold story inside you." – Maya Angelou.

Life has a way of throwing unexpected challenges our way, testing our strength and resilience. Sometimes, these challenges come in the form of small disappointments, and other times, they cut deeper — leaving scars that aren't always visible.

But when someone breaks your spirit or shatters your peace, it's like breaking a bird's wings. You can't just anticipate that it would fly again without a struggle. The pain doesn't simply vanish overnight; it stays hidden beneath the surface, affecting every step forward.

They say when you break a bird's wings, you can't expect it to fly. The same goes for people. When you break a child's smile or spirit, you can't expect that child to laugh and move on as if nothing happened. You can't shatter someone's soul and their inner peace and expect them to wake up the next day and go on like it's a normal day.

Abusers often set these expectations for their victims — be it their children, their spouses, or anyone they mistreat. They act like everything should go back to normal as if the pain they've caused can simply be ignored or forgotten. But that's not how it works. The wounds don't just disappear. The scars never fully fade.

You either choose to face your trauma, fight it every single day, or you live with it. Either way, it affects your life. It changes you. And people should never feel ashamed to talk about their traumas or the pain they've endured, no matter what our culture says. Everyone has the right to share their truth, to heal, and to fight for their own peace.

The Complicated Grief of Losing an Abusive Parent

We often find ourselves carrying burdens that were never ours to bear, especially when it comes to family. The people who are supposed to protect and care for us, our parents, can sometimes be the ones who hurt us the most. In many cultures, as in Islam, in terms of respect, the parents are placed after God. The Quran mentions the mother three times before it even brings up the father. So, for many of us, confronting our parents feels unthinkable. I could never look my mother in the eye and say, "You did this to me. You caused me pain." And I never once expected my father to say, "I'm sorry." That's just not something that would ever happen. For the longest time, I simply accepted that.

But at 50, I had a wake-up call. I realized that the pain was swallowing me whole, and I decided to take a step toward healing. But here's the thing—healing isn't a magic cure. You don't just "get over it." It's messy, it's hard, and it's ongoing. You learn to live with it, to make peace with the scars.

That's why I decided to write this book. To tell anyone out there who feels like they're alone in their pain that they aren't. To say that it's okay to talk about it. Talking helps. It doesn't erase the past, but it makes the weight a little easier to carry.

When my father died, my grief was complicated. I didn't just mourn him; I mourned the father he never was, the peace I never felt around him. It wasn't just the loss that broke my heart, but the fear of what lay ahead for his soul. I don't know where he's headed, but from what I know of him and his actions, I'm afraid. I dare not say he's destined for peace; only God knows. And that thought, that worry, breaks my heart. So, I pray for him. I give Zakat, hoping it might help his soul in the afterlife.

Despite everything, I still love him. And that might be hard to understand, but it's true. Ask anyone who has been hurt by the people they love—they'll tell you the same. Love doesn't disappear just because it's mixed with pain. We love our parents because that's what's in our hearts, even when those hearts are bruised and battered. I'm angry at what he did to me, but that anger doesn't erase the love. It just makes everything so much more complicated.

My father was an alcoholic, and we watched him slowly fall apart over the years. There was no hope of him getting better—no good days, no sign of healing, just a steady decline. I remember being a young child, maybe around two, when I first understood that something wasn't right with him. From then on, until the day he passed away in January 2018, it was always the same: a downward spiral that seemed to have no end.

He went from having everything to having nothing. From a man of means to one who lost it all—his home, his pride, his dignity. He never let go of the alcohol or the cigarettes. He never let go of the things that dragged him deeper into that dark place. And he seemed to accept it as if he'd made peace with his own destruction. No matter what anyone did or said, he seemed almost content with the life he had chosen.

He'd drop by for a meal now and then or bring my mom some laundry he couldn't wash wherever he was staying. In the last ten years of his life, he had no real home. He moved from place to place—his brother's house, a friend's couch, anywhere he could find a bed for the night. He lost the sense of pride and dignity he once had when he had money, and somehow, he seemed okay with that.

We tried to help him, but he refused. No matter what kind of support we offered, he never took it. I saw my father lose everything, but the saddest part was that he didn't seem to care. And in some ways, I think that hurt the most—knowing that he had given up long before we did.

While my family was still in Tunisia and I had already moved to Dubai, we received some shocking news about my father. A driver who had once worked for us called my brother, saying that my father had been found lying on the floor in a room somewhere and had contracted an illness. We had no idea—life was going on as usual for us, and this news hit hard.

My brother, acting quickly, arranged for him to be transported to Tunisia. He got him admitted into a luxurious, top-tier retirement home for the elderly, sparing no expense to ensure he received the best possible care. Despite this, my father fought against the help he was being given.

Denied both alcohol and cigarettes, he was pushed over the edge. He would ask us to take him out of the facility, saying that he only wanted his drink and cigarettes. Obviously, the staff at the facility and my brother didn't comply with his demands.

However, his health kept declining. He suffered a major blow when his kidneys failed, and then soon after, various other diseases started taking their toll. Ultimately, he passed away only at the age of 72. I remember receiving a call from my sister, telling me that Baba had passed away. I didn't know how to feel. A part of me was shocked, but deep down, I knew it was going to happen. I accepted it even though I was heartbroken for him.

I couldn't stop myself from wondering where he was now. What had become of him? Was he at peace? In some way, maybe he was, and it was for the best. It was devastating for us to watch him decline and accept the way his life was. Seeing him refuse help and continue on the path of self-destruction was heartbreaking. In the end, the greatest sorrow was knowing he couldn't let go of his vices, even when help was within reach.

Dealing with an alcoholic is a different kind of struggle—one where forgiveness and negotiations often don't work. When I think about my father, I see a man who was content with his downward spiral. He didn't want to take responsibility or improve his situation. He was fine moving from a lavish life in Paris and Monte Carlo to living in a single room at his brother's place. As long as he had his bottle of alcohol, he seemed content with his lot in life.

We tried to keep up appearances, hiding the reality from our friends and family, presenting a façade that he was still the dignified, elegant man he once was. But the truth was, he had settled into a life of rags and was perfectly okay with it. For the longest time, I tried to keep my ex-husband and daughter from seeing the truth. I didn't want them to notice the difference between the life we projected and the life he was living.

Sadly, you cannot argue or bring a change in a person who's so deeply ingrained in their way. My father had accepted his situation, and he was fine with it – there was only so much we could do.

We made sure to be there for him, financially or physically, should he need us. My siblings and I did everything in our hands to help him get better. But deep down, we knew it was a lost cause. He would happily live on the streets as long as he had his alcohol.

It took us long enough to understand his mindset. We finally accepted that this battle wasn't worth fighting. If he didn't see the wrong in his actions, what choice did we have other than to accept him as he was? It was painful, but we knew it was all we could do.

Healing from Within

I had this anger building up inside me for years, and it made me upset. I didn't want to be angry anymore. All I want is to be happy. Really happy. But happiness can only come from within ourselves. Yet, it's easier said than done. Sometimes, it's incredibly challenging to find that happiness.

When you've been going through challenge after challenge, you suddenly start hearing this voice inside you. "I want to make it. I want to move on. I want to be happy." It begs you to move on and find your happiness. In reality, you can never really move on.

The pain is always there, deeply buried. It follows you everywhere you go. Still, it's not worth living in the shadows of the trauma. Why let it keep you unhappy? That's why I chose to look for happiness. It doesn't matter if I have to chase it; I'll follow it regardless of where it leads me.

I find it in the small things, like seeing a smile on my daughter's face and feeling the warmth of her laughter. I want every day to be a little bit better than the last. I want to move forward to make my days count, and that's what keeps me going. That makes me happy.

I've also learned to stop judging others and, more importantly, to stop judging myself. It's not about forgiving or forgetting because some things are too deep to ever truly forgive or forget. You can't just erase the moments when someone broke you. And yes, I've been broken, like so many others, but I've realized something important: healing is a personal journey. No one can do it for you. You have to go inside yourself, face the darkness, and find a way to let in the light.

After everything we went through, my mother became my closest friend. As we moved from Libya to Tunis and then to Istanbul, we leaned on each other. It was like we were on a team, working together to handle the ups and downs of life.

My mother, despite everything she suffered, turned into my best friend. She was always there for me, even when life was hard. I understood her struggles and admired her strength. She is more than just a parent; she is a vital part of my life.

I begin my days by calling my mom – my good morning call. Following my morning ritual, I listen to the Quran. Our daily routine keeps us close. We now care for her as she once cared for us, and she's become an amazing grandmother to my daughter. Her love and kindness never falter, no matter what.

Life and its challenges have only brought us closer. My mother's love is a constant source of comfort, no matter where I am. She's my healing, my strength, and my reminder that love can mend even the deepest wounds.

When we first moved to Tripoli, Libya, and were staying in that motel after leaving Beirut, I had a major emotional outburst. It was one of those moments where you say things you regret later. I remember yelling at my mother and then walking out of the room. She followed me, listened to me, and wrapped me in a hug.

That moment was a turning point for us. For the first time, it felt like she truly saw me and understood what I was going through. Over time, she would share with me how she knew what I was dealing with that she understood because I reminded her of herself. She never denied my pain nor my struggles.

There are countless moments like that where her love and understanding helped me heal. It wasn't about forgiving or forgetting; it was about her being there, showing me that love can be the most powerful form of healing.

Pushing Myself to Do My Best

Every day, I wake up with a goal: to be better than I was yesterday. I push myself to do my best in everything I do—whether it's my faith, my family, or my friends. For me, there's no in-between; it's all or nothing. I strive to leave behind the anger and emotional turmoil of my past because it's not worth it—neither for my health nor for my soul.

I care deeply about how others see me. I want to be remembered as a good person, so I focus on doing good and being kind. I teach my daughter the same values because I believe nothing else truly matters.

My faith is a significant part of this journey. I pray often, listen to the Quran, and seek peace within myself. I constantly worry about the afterlife and focus on my goal to enter paradise. I understand this might not be everyone's belief. However, to me, it is my aim. Life is short, and I don't want to waste it on the wrong path.

While far from perfect, I try my best to be pure and good at heart. If I unintentionally do wrong to someone, I immediately apologize with sincerity. In fact, I feel a pang of guilt for accidentally hurting an ant. That's how I heal. Being pure and kind helps me heal. I came out of that storm not as someone broken or filled with anger but as someone stronger and better. That strength was always inside me; I just had to choose to embrace it.

When life gets tough, we have a choice. Let those hardships turn us into a bitter, judgemental person who seeks revenge or take the high road and take it as an opportunity to become a better person.

I chose to be better. Every story I've shared, and every trauma I've faced has been a lesson in self-growth. I've learned to forgive myself when I fall short, to make amends, and to continually work on improving myself.

It all starts from within. You have to genuinely want to change and grow. I want that for myself. I refuse to be ashamed of my past, and no one should be ashamed of theirs, either. Whether you've been a victim, made mistakes, or done wrong, owning up to it and striving to make things right is what truly matters. None of us are perfect. We come into this world with flaws, and life will test us in ways we never expect.

The key is to acknowledge our flaws and decide whether we'll let them define us or work to overcome them. I chose the latter. I faced my flaws, learned from them, and made the decision to improve. That's the journey I'm on, and it's a journey worth taking.

Why I Wrote This Book

Even though writing about my experiences hasn't been easy, they were an eye-opener for sure. This book helped me realize that I have made it through the other side stronger than before. Sure, I may not be completely healed yet, but I've come a long way. And if I can do it, so can you.

We all have an inner strength, but it's up to us to either find and harness it or let it stay buried forever. Allah tests our patience and resilience, and that's why he puts us in these situations. You could be facing a conflict, dealing with a trauma, or struggling financially right now, but believe me, it will get better. Our responses to such adversities matter more than you think. It's our choices that help us get through such ordeals.

Not so long ago, I promised myself I would become a better person, not for myself, but for my daughter. I want to become her ideal, her role model. I want her to think about me and say, "I want to be like my mother." Thus, I make sure my resilience and faith never falter, no matter what I go through.

You might be wondering, 'Oh, she makes it sound so easy.' I understand it's not as easy as it looks. But what choice do we have? We can only face our challenges head-on to turn those struggles into stepping stones towards a better future, a better version of ourselves.

Let my story be a reminder for you, dear reader. A reminder that you're not alone. We all go through tough times, some more than others. However, I always need you to remember that your pain isn't isolated. There's someone out there who shares your suffering, whether you're dealing with mental health issues, job loss, relationship problems, or other challenges.

I've been lucky to have great people in my life—my sister, my brother, my daughter, my mother, and even my ex-husband, who helped me more than he probably knows. Good people make a big difference, and I hope you have such support, too.

This book is a reminder that there's no shame in going through tough times. It doesn't matter if you've faced abuse, regretful actions, or other difficulties; it's crucial to remember that we're all part of a community. By sharing our stories, we help each other heal and move forward.

Every person we meet has their own story. I hope mine helps you feel a bit less alone. If you see parts of yourself in my experiences, know that I've been through it, too. We all have our unique paths, but together, we can support one another and find strength in our shared experiences.

Whenever I have to make a decision, I jump right in. I don't wait for fear and hesitation to hold me back. If you sit around letting fear take over, you'll simply remain stuck in the same place. And that's a trap I wouldn't wish on anyone.

So, when it comes to making choices, always dive in headfirst. Fear may try to get the best of you, but don't let it take control. Remember, if you're scared, it's the best time to take the leap. Don't allow negative feelings to paralyze you because staying in an endless cycle is far worse than taking a risk.

I've also grown to trust my intuition and decisions over time. I've started following what feels right in my gut, and that's something that really helped me find a clear and fulfilling path. It doesn't overcomplicate things unnecessarily, and that's precisely what you need to make your life change for the better.

Your gut feeling and intuition are powerful tools. They'll tell you when you're on the right track or when you need to rethink things. I've found that when I listen to my heart and instincts, I can move forward with confidence and find success. So, I encourage you to trust your own inner guidance—it's more reliable than you might think.

What It Means to Be Vulnerable

I first worked with the UNHCR in 1996. At that time, I lived in Beirut, Lebanon. After having moved to Tripoli, Libya, I continued to work for them. Since then, I've been connected to them as a volunteer. Throughout these years, I've helped countless refugees in need and witnessed heart-wrenching stories – from abused women to suffering children and men.

The sad part is the help they receive is often far from enough. Having lost everything, refugees are the most vulnerable people. They have nothing to call their own except for the inner strength they possess. It urges them to keep going. For some reason, their struggles always struck a chord in my heart because, in a way, I know what it feels like to be displaced. To lose a home.

My family and I have been forced to evacuate our homes multiple times – sometimes even in the middle of the night. We would be left stranded with no directions or resources. In fact, there were times when my father would push us out. Knowing how it feels makes me empathize with those people. Even though I can't step into their shoes fully, the least I can offer is my support and understanding.

It is due to my time at the UNHCR that I had the idea of writing this book. I want the world to know what it really means to be vulnerable – whether you are a refugee, someone dealing with trauma, or anyone who's been abused.

I might appear completely normal on the outside, but as you know by now, my life has been riddled with challenges. I hope reading my story can offer you comfort if you're going through the same tough times. Remember, every smile hides a story, and not all of those stories are easy or pleasant to hear.

Trauma and pain are like generational curses that overshadow us like an invisible weight. I've seen people avoid it and pretend everything is fine. If you're trying to normalize the pain you feel and hoping for it to fade away with time, you're mistaken. Take it from someone who's been there. That's not how it works. Avoiding trauma simply means robbing ourselves of a chance to really heal.

I'm different. In my family, I'm the one who does not shy away from feeling the pain. I feel deeply. I don't consider it as a weakness. I consider it as a gift.

While my siblings might find comfort in their avoidance, thinking everything is okay because they don't confront the pain, I refuse to do the same. I choose to fully experience my pain, no matter how messy or uncomfortable it is. Some might call it imbalance or suggest I have too many issues. But for me, feeling my pain is part of the healing process. It's how I work through it, how I grow, and ultimately, how I heal.

Letting Go of What You Can't Change

You may not realize this right now, but life's twists and turns can imbed you with incredible strength. While you find your way around those challenges, you're learning to balance your feelings and see things more clearly – beyond your personal perspective. It helps you figure out what's worth your mental health and what's not.

Over time, I've learned that not everything is worth stress and heartache. I should value my mental health and prioritize it over every pain or trauma I have experienced. We all have just one life, so make sure to keep your well-being above everything else.

As you grow mature, you also start seeing people for who they truly are. It doesn't matter if you just met them or have known them your entire life; you become capable of seeing what's beneath the surface.

You learn that you can't change their thoughts, behaviours, or actions, no matter how much you want to. Just as you can't force someone to drink water if they're not thirsty, you can't force people to think or act differently if they're not ready or willing.

It's a tough lesson but one that's essential for your own peace of mind. You might feel like you need to mold others to fit your expectations but remember, it's always better to let go. Don't push hard. People will be who they are, and you can't force them to change unless they want to.

I noticed a change in myself when I began prioritizing my mental health. I was a different person altogether. A person who doesn't let others affect her sense of peace or contentment. A person who values herself. A person who is concerned about herself more than anything else.

Trust me, you never have to pretend to have it all together and put on a happy, brave smile. Sure, that's what people expect, but why do we let people dictate how we should act? I want you to know that it's perfectly fine to be real. It's alright to admit if you're not okay. It's okay to accept your trauma and allow yourself to feel upset.

Looking back, I believe I'm not as kind or trustworthy as I used to be. But I'm not ashamed of admitting that. Why would I be? I've learned to have faith in my feelings and instincts. Overcomplicating things in my head or trusting others more than required has never brought any good into my life.

Granted, I learned this the hard way, but the truth is, not everyone has your best interests at heart. I mean, if you're lucky, you may have a good mother, supportive children, or caring friends. However, in the real world, people are usually focused on their own lives. At the end of the day, it's just you against the entire world.

So, I don't recommend pretending to be constantly positive or happy. Just take a moment to be honest with yourself and others about where you are. Value simplicity. Trust me, simplifying my thoughts and life has brought me so much peace.

For me now, finding happiness means embracing simplicity and being honest about my feelings. It's about accepting that it's okay not to be okay sometimes.

For so long, I tried to present myself as this perfect person—smart, happy, and always okay. I wanted everyone to see me as having it all together. But pretending that everything was perfect only made things worse inside me. It's more important to admit when we're not okay. It's okay to have traumas, to feel ungrateful sometimes, or to just not feel blessed, even if everything around us seems fine.

Learning to Simplify Life

We live in a world that tells us we need to look a certain way, act a certain way, and have certain goals. But honestly, we all have our own struggles. We work to make ends meet, to find shelter, and to ensure we have enough to eat. But does that truly make us happy? It's important to have these basics, but beyond that, happiness often comes from simplicity.

Simplifying our surroundings, our lives, and our expectations can help us find peace. Happiness doesn't need to be complicated. It's about being okay with who you are and accepting that it's okay not to be okay. It's about shedding the shame of our past and looking forward with a clear, honest perspective.

After a lifetime of ups and downs—of love, hate, shouting, and fighting—I've finally learned the art of communication. It's something so many people underestimate, but it's crucial for every relationship in our lives. I didn't always know how to communicate effectively. Coming from a home filled with violence and anger, I only knew how to shout and argue. It got me nowhere, only pushed people away and left me feeling angry and sad.

But I've taken a step back, breathed deeply, and worked hard to learn how to communicate calmly and peacefully. This change has brought me so much peace. Now, I'm proud at the end of each day, knowing that the people I love—my mother, my sister, my daughter, and my brother—are happy with me. I go to bed feeling content because I've simplified my life and embraced the basics.

Never underestimate the power of good communication and simple, positive interactions. I've learned to simplify my life, to cherish having a roof over my head, and to appreciate the small blessings. Working with UNHCR has given me perspective on the struggles of refugees, but it also reminds me of how fortunate I am to have stability.

The road hasn't been easy, and there's still more to come, but I'm proud of the incredible young woman I've raised. It's not about being told to be resilient or strong all the time. It's about being okay with saying, "I'm not okay," and accepting that it's fine to be imperfect. Simplify your life, accept where you are, and be kind to yourself.

We're not alone in our struggles. Most people face similar issues—whether it's family problems, trauma, or abuse. Many people choose to avoid these issues, but I've never wanted to live in avoidance. I want to be true to my feelings and to myself.

I choose simplicity and honesty. I want to face my emotions, not hide from them. And it's okay.

www.ingramcontent.com/pod-product-compliance
Lightning Source LLC
Chambersburg PA
CBHW070758050426
42452CB00012B/2397